GOGURYEO

In Search of Its Culture and History

Korean History

GOGURYEO

In Search of Its Culture and History

by Ho-tae Jeon

 Hollym

Goguryeo: In Search of Its Culture and History

Korea Foundation
한국국제교류재단

The Korea Foundation has provided financial assistance
for the undertaking of this publication project.

First published in 2008
Second printing, 2012
by Hollym International Corp., USA
Phone 908 353 1655   **Fax** 908 353 0255
http://www.hollym.com   **e-Mail** contact@hollym.com

 Hollym

Published simultaneously in Korea
by Hollym Corp., Publishers, Seoul, Korea
Phone +82 2 734 5087   **Fax** +82 2 730 5149
http://www.hollym.co.kr   **e-Mail** info@hollym.co.kr

ISBN: 978-1-56591-282-3
Library of Congress Control Number: 2008937888

Printed in Korea

* Romanization of Korean names in this book follows the Romanization system
  used by the Korean government since 2000.

Preface

Goguryeo was not only the leader during the Korea's Three Kingdoms Period but also the representative of the ancient Northeast Asia. Much of Goguryeo's culture became part of Korean culture, but it also became the origin of Northeast Asian culture. Thus, Goguryeo's history and culture is an important key to understanding the ancient Korea as well as the ancient Northeast Asia as whole.

This book summarizes Goguryeo's history and culture for a general audience. I tried to describe Goguryeo's 700 year-old history as a development of Goguryeo as a specific nation and as a part of East Asia.

I explained each categories of Goguryeo culture with the evidence of Goguryeo tomb murals, artifacts and sites. Through this book, the readers can comprehend the characteristics of Goguryeo culture: the individuality based on diversity, universality with originality, openness with selectivity. I organized the data so that the readers can understand not only food, clothing and housing, but also architecture, music, art, entertainment, sports, faith, religion, myth, astronomy and other concepts and ideas of Goguryeo people.

Although the readers cannot directly experience Goguryeo people's life, I hope they can get familiar with Goguryeo through the various historical sources and explanations in the book. Also, I hope the readers familiarize with history and culture of Goguryeo people, who were open to new culture and eager to merge the old and new to create original Goguryeo.

I want to thank all of those who helped me write this book. Especially, I want to give thanks to my wife Yeon-hee Jang, who helped adjust the contents for general audience, Jeong-hyeon Yi, who revised the English text, and my daughter Hye-jeon Jeon. My thanks to Chan-soo Park and Kyung-hee Lee of Hollym Corp., Publishers who helped publish the book. And thanks to Hye-joon Jeon, who always encourages his father.

Ho-tae Jeon

Contents

I

Life and Culture of the Goguryeo People

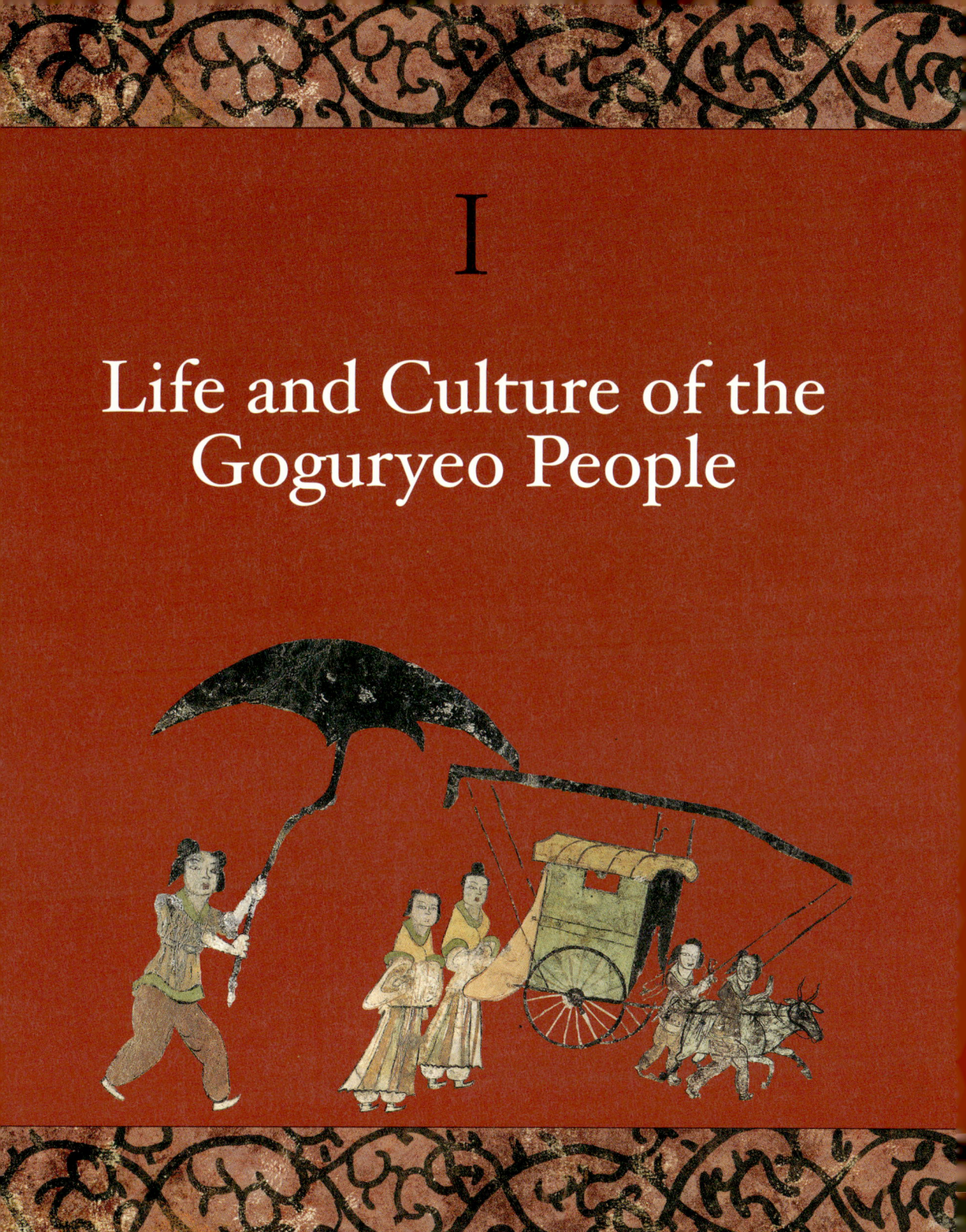

Life of Goguryeo Aristocrats in Fifth-Century Pyeongyang

1

In the fifth century, the East Asian region witnessed an active exchange of culture and goods amid a stable international order. Major cities in Goguryeo imported the cultures and goods of central and western Asia via the Southern and Northern Dynasties (南北朝) of China as well as the Turks (突厥) of inner Asia. Buddhism from India was also embraced. Unique for having integrated a variety of cultural imports, Goguryeo in the late fifth century influenced the neighboring countries of Silla (新羅), Baekje (百濟) and Wae (倭, Japan) and created a Pan-Goguryeo culture sphere within Northeast Asia.

Goguryeo aristocrats living in Pyeongyang, the center of this cosmopolitan culture, enjoyed a variety of social and cultural benefits. When the state moved the capital from Gungnaeseong (國內城) to Pyeongyang in 427, Pyeongyangseong Fortress (平壤城) was built on flat terrain, and Daeseong

Mountain Fortress (大城山城) constructed on the surrounding Mt. Daeseongsan. In the sixth century, a new fortress called Janganseong (長安城) was erected to encircle the city of Pyeongyang (fig. 1). Janganseong was divided into outer, middle, inner and north fortresses, taking advantage of the Botonggang river (普通江), Daedonggang river (大同江), Moranbong peak (牡丹峯) and other mountain peaks. The aristocrats lived in commodious residences inside the outer fortress; administrative offices were situated in the middle fortress, and the royal palace in the inner fortress (fig. 2).

Fig. 1. Map of Janganseong Fortress
(Pyeongyang, North Korea)

Fig. 2-1. Gatekeepers(replica)
(Mural on the eastern and western sides of the north wall of the antechamber's entrance,
Ssangyeongchong in Nampo, North Korea)

Fig. 2-2. Gatekeepers
(Mural on the northern and southern sides of the east wall of the antechamber's entrance,
Jangcheon Tomb No.1 in Ji'an, China)

13

Fig. 3-1. *Giwa* ↑
(Korean roof-end tile from Pyeongyang, Seoul National University Museum)

Fig. 3-2. *Byeokdol* ↗
(Korean brick from Pyeongyang, Seoul National University Museum)

Located within the outer fortress, aristocratic residences featured roofs covered with Korean roof-end tiles (fig. 3), and rooms equipped with a heating system called *ondol*(溫突) (fig. 4). Many facilities were found inside these residences (fig. 5): the men's quarters called *sarangchae* that included a stable, warehouse, and servants' quarters; and the women's quarters called *anchae*, which included a kitchen, storage rooms for meat and grain, mill, a well and a pond. The master's wife stayed in the *anchae* and ran the household, while the master oversaw his affairs and received guests in the *sarangchae* (fig. 6-7).

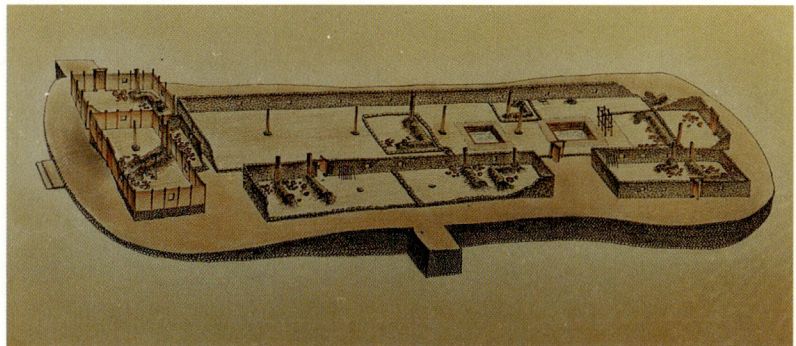

Fig. 4. Reconstruction of *ondol* site
(Fort No.4 on Mt. Achasan in Seoul, Choi, Jong-taek)

Fig. 5. Aristocratic residence
(Mural on the west wall of the burial chamber, Anak Tomb No. 1 in Anak, North Korea)

Fig. 6-1. Thirteen magistrates paying respects to the tomb occupant
(Mural on the west wall of the antechamber, Deokheung-ri Mural Tomb in Nampo, North Korea)

Fig. 6-2. Governor of Yuju ↑
(Mural on the north wall of the antechamber,
Deokheung-ri Mural Tomb in Nampo, North Korea)

Fig. 6-3. Tomb occupant ←
(Mural on the north wall of the burial chamber,
Deokheung-ri Mural Tomb in Nampo, North Korea)

Fig. 7-1. Battle-ax warriors
(Mural on the lower part of the eastern side of the antechamber's south wall,
Anak Tomb No. 3 in Anak, North Korea)

Fig. 7-2. Standard-bearers
(Mural on the upper part of the eastern side of the antechamber's south wall,
Anak Tomb No. 3 in Anak, North Korea)

Fig. 7-3. Tomb occupant
(Mural on the west wall of the
western side chamber attached to
the antechamber, Anak Tomb
No. 3 in Anak, North Korea)

Fig. 7-4. Tomb occupant's wife and her servants
(Mural on the north wall of the western side chamber attached to the antechamber,
Anak Tomb No. 3 in Anak, North Korea)

Fig. 7-5. Tomb occupant and his wives (replica)
(Mural on the northeast wall of the burial chamber, (original) Gakjeochong in Ji'an, China; Sookmyung Women's University)

Fig. 7-6. Tomb occupant and his wife
(Mural on the north wall of the burial chamber, Ssangyeongchong in Nampo, North Korea)

The gardens in the residence served as a site for military training, games and plays such as *masahui*(馬射戲). The master often invited performance troupes to act, sing or play music. On outings, aristocrats were accompanied by guards whose number was determined by the individual's social status [fig. 8]. Aristocrats enjoyed performance or sporting events from the front row in ox-drawn carriages. Among the popular combative sports were *subakhui*(手搏戲) and *ssireum*, a type of Korean wrestling.

Fig. 8-1. Grand Procession
(Corridor mural, northern and eastern sides of the burial chamber, Anak Tomb No. 3 in Anak, North Korea)

Fig. 8-2. Outing of the tomb occupant and his wife
(Mural on the west wall of the burial chamber, Susan-ri Mural Tomb in Nampo, North Korea)

Some aristocrats invited monks into their residences to conduct Buddhist sermons and ceremonies such as *chilbo gongyang* (七寶供養, offering seven treasures to Buddha) during which they prayed for entrance into the Buddhist paradise called *jeongto* (淨土) **(fig. 9)**. In contrast, their wives often visited Buddhist temples in person to pray. As many considered the lotus flower a symbol of Buddhist ideology and paradise, aristocrats often requested that their tombs be decorated in lotus flower motifs. Frequently, aristocrats donated property in order to construct temples, pagodas or Buddhist statues.

The life of commoners was far more arduous. After the farming season, they were then subjected to corvee labor — repairing roads or building fortresses —, which made their off-season more difficult. They were also obligated to enlist as soldiers whenever the kingdom went to war. Often those who did not own land sold valued commodities like salt or simple arts and crafts as a way to support their families. Those who lacked special skills were forced to work as servants in aristocratic households. As for leisure, the performances in the Dongmaeng (東盟) festival or village rituals were the only entertainment enjoyed by commoners.

Fig. 9. Offering ceremony of the seven treasures to Buddha
(Mural on the east wall of the burial chamber, Deokheung-ri Mural Tomb in Nampo, North Korea)

2 Housing

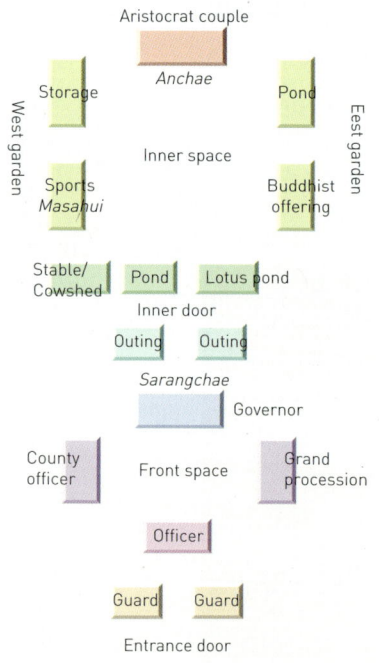

Aristocrat couple

Anchae

Storage   Pond

West garden   East garden

Inner space

Sports *Masahui*   Buddhist offering

Stable/Cowshed   Pond   Lotus pond

Inner door

Outing   Outing

Sarangchae

Governor

County officer   Front space   Grand procession

Officer

Guard   Guard

Entrance door

Fig. 10. Aristocratic residence
(Reconstruction from murals of
Deokheung-ri Mural Tomb in Nampo,
North Korea)

Goguryeo aristocratic residences consisted of an outer men's quarters (*sarangchae*) and an inner women's quarters (*anchae*) with an inner gate between the two buildings (fig. 10). The *sarangchae* was used for receiving guests while the *anchae* was reserved for the family and everyday chores. In addition to the main residence rooms and kitchen, there were other adjacent buildings such as stables and mills. Murals from Anak Tomb No. 3 and the Yaksu-ri Mural Tomb depict the internal structure of aristocratic homes in detail. Notably, the cooking fire pit and chimney in the kitchens, are built at right angles, in contrast to the parallel arrangements used in China. This is a unique form seen only in

Goguryeo. A glazed stove similar to the one described in the murals was excavated in Maseongu Tomb No. 1 in Ji'an, China. The houses depicted in the murals share some similarities with those found in today's Korean farming villages: cooking areas upon which earthenware steamers hung; small meal tables with rake-shaped legs; wells with buckets in the yard; treadmills; two-storied storages; and oxen with rings in their noses (fig. 11).

Fig. 11-1. Kitchen and meat storehouse
(Mural on the east wall of the eastern side chamber attached to the antechamber, Anak Tomb No. 3 in Anak, North Korea)

Fig. 11-2. Carriage Shed →
(Mural on the east wall of the
eastern side chamber attached to
the antechamber, Anak Tomb No. 3
in Anak, North Korea)

Fig. 11-3. Well ↘
(Mural on the north wall of the
eastern side chamber attached to
the antechamber, Anak Tomb No. 3
in Anak, North Korea)

Fig. 11-4. Mill ←
(Mural on the west wall of the eastern side chamber attached to the antechamber, Anak Tomb No. 3 in Anak, North Korea)

Fig. 11-5. Cowshed ╱
(Mural on the south wall of the eastern side chamber attached to the antechamber, Anak Tomb No. 3 in Anak, North Korea)

Fig. 11-6. Stable
(Mural on the west wall of the
eastern side chamber attached
to the antechamber, Anak
Tomb No. 3 ın Anak, North
Korea)

Fig. 11-7. Stable and cowshed
(Mural on the south wall of the
burial chamber, Deokheung-ri
Mural Tomb in Nampo, North
Korea)

Inside the house, low benches called *pyeongsang* (平床) (fig. 12) and chairs with long legs called *jwasang* (座床) were used. *Pyeongsang* is wider than *jwasang* but with short legs to make the seat closer to the heated floor. In addition, murals at the Gakjeochong and Muyongchong tombs confirm that *jwasang* was used in places like the living room (fig. 13).

Archaeological excavations indicate that the floor heating system known as *ondol* originated in Gojoseon. During the Goguryeo period, the *ondol* system evolved to become one of the main elements in the construction of a house. The Goguryeo people, who had to withstand the cold winters, heated a portion of the clay floor to sustain the room's heat. Excavated remnants of the early *ondol* system include either a straight flue (一) or bent flue (ㄱ) that was affixed to the floor. When a fire was built at the end of the flue, the heat and smoke passed through the flue and emerged at the other end through a chimney. The heat rising from the fire fueled by dried branches and other materials warmed the flat stone above the flue, which in turn heated up the clay floor. As the warm air rose, colder air fell to the ground to be warmed by the heated floor, thus heating the room.

Fig. 12. *Pyeongsang*
(Mural on the ceiling corbels of the burial chamber, Muyongchong in Ji'an, China)

Fig. 13. *Jwasang*
(Mural on the northeast wall of the burial chamber, Muyongchong in Ji'an, China)

Fig. 14. *Ondol*
(Fort No. 4 on Mt. Achasan in Seoul, Korea)

Goguryeo's *ondol* sytem can be identified in the ruins of Dongtaizi (東坮子) in Ji'an, China and Omae-ri Jeolgol in Hamgyeongnam-do province in North Korea (fig. 14). This type of *ondol* system was revealed in a recent excavation of a Goguryeo fort located on Mt. Achasan in Seoul. Goguryeo's neighbors — northern China to the west and Silla and Baekje to the south used the system. after adapting it to their particular climate and lifestyle. Since *ondol* construction required special expertise and considerable cost, it was used only in the royal palaces, temples, administrative offices, and residences of aristocrats. Commoners rarely used the *ondol* system, and when they did, only heated a small portion of the floor.

Clothing 3

Garments

The attire of the Goguryeo people can be ascertained more easily from murals than from descriptions in documents. According to these drawings, nomadic tribes of inner Asia shared the same style of attire with the Goguryeo people. Men typically wore a jacket called *jeogori* and pants called *baji* (fig. 15). They also wore outer garments, belts, head ornaments and headwear and shoes. Women's clothes were very similar to those of men with the addition of a long, wide skirt called *chima* (fig. 16).

Fig. 15-1. Man
(Mural on the south wall of the first burial chamber, Samsilchong in Ji'an, China)

Fig. 15-2. Man
(Mural on the west wall of the antechamber, Deokheung-ri Mural Tomb in Nampo, North Korea)

Fig. 15-3. Man
(Mural on the north wall of the burial chamber, Susan-ri Mural Tomb in Nampo, North Korea)

Fig. 16-1. Woman →
(Mural on the west wall of the burial chamber, Susan-ri Mural Tomb in Nampo, North Korea)

Fig. 16-2. Woman ↓
(Mural on the south wall of the first burial chamber, Samsilchong in Ji'an, China)

Fig. 16-3. Woman ↘
(Mural on the north wall of the burial chamber, Deokheung-ri Mural Tomb in Nampo, North Korea)

Fig. 17. Weaving woman (replica)
(Mural on the south wall of the burial chamber, Daean-ri Tomb No.1 in Nampo, North Korea)

The materials, colors, girth of pants or skirts, *seon* (trim) decoration and pattern of clothes differed according to social status, class and region. Aristocrats wore long and roomy colorful silk garments imprinted with showy patterns. In contrast, in order to facilitate ease of movement, commoners wore tight clothing made of plain fabrics in monotonous colors. *Jajihilmungeum* (紫地詰文錦), *osaekgeum* (五色錦), and *unpogeum* (雲布錦) are representative of the high quality of silk woven in Goguryeo. A Goguryeo loom was depicted in

Maseongu Tomb No. 1 and in Daean-ri Tomb No. 1 that showed a woman weaving fabric seated in front of a loom (fig. 17).

Even within Goguryeo, detailed differences in attire can be seen between the Ji'an and Pyeongyang regions. In the Ji'an area, dots, single diamond shapes or flower patterns were repeated on simple, brightly colored fabric. But in Pyeongyang, two or three patterns among clouds, waves, vines, and various geometric shapes were printed on a variety of more brilliantly colored fabrics. This difference in fashion can be attributed to the fact that the Ji'an area continued to use the colors originally prevalent in Goguryeo while the region around the capital Pyeongyang had accepted the culture of China.

For men, the jacket was initially fastened left to right but later on was fastened from right to left. The jacket just covered the waist, while the ends of the sleeves and collar, and the lower hem of the jacket were trimmed with a narrow band named *seon*(襈) that was made of a different color of fabric. As for the outer garment, men wore a long coat called *durumagi* for official occasions and *deot jeogori* layered over the jacket for ordinary occasions. There were two types of coat arrangements: *mat yeomim* (straight opening) and *eogim yeomim* (directional opening: left or right). There were also two types of belts: one that used only fabric, colorful thread and leather, and the other with gold, silver and metal ornaments hung over the fabric or leather belt.

For Goguryeo women, jackets and pants did not differ significantly from those of men in terms of form, usage and features. The long, wide skirt had pleats and *seon* at the end. Its length varied, falling either to the shins or feet. Women also wore long coats that were trimmed at the sleeves and collar with *seon* and extended slightly below the jacket. The coat's belt varied in color — black, white, red, purple or light green — and was adorned with triangular or flower-shaped ornaments.

Hats and Shoes

Men usually wore their hair in a single topknot. The types of headwear included hoods, *jeolpung* (折風), *chaek* (幘), *gwan* (冠), and *paeraengi* (bamboo hats), etc. (fig. 18). Everyone regardless of status and class wore black hoods and *paeraengi*, but commoners most often wore hoods. *Jeolpung* is a cone-shaped hat with a black brim, a white veil that covers the forehead, and ribbons at both sides. Depending on status, the *jeolpung*

Fig. 18-1. *Gwan*
(Mural on the north wall of the
burial chamber, Deokheung-ri
Mural Tomb
in Nampo, North Korea)

Fig. 18-2. *Chaek*
(Mural on the west wall of the
antechamber, Deokheung-ri
Mural Tomb in Nampo, North
Korea)

Fig. 18-3. *Chaek*
(Corridor mural, eastern side of
the burial chamber, Anak Tomb
No. 3 in Anak, North Korea)

Fig. 18-4. *Jeolpung*
(Mural on the southeast wall of the
burial chamber, Muyongchong
in Ji'an, China)

Fig. 18-5. *Jeolpung*
(Mural on the south wall of the
first burial chamber, Samsilchong
in Ji'an, China)

had feathers or metal ornaments on both sides. All public officials wore *chaek*: civil officials donned three-horned *chaek*, while military officials wore *chaek* with an elevated peak. Goguryeo's *chaek* differed from that of China as the Chinese *chaek* draped a cloth called *su* (收) on the back of the hat. *Gwan* was loosely woven out of *na* (羅), a type of silk. Kings wore white hats, ministers blue ones, and high-ranking aristocrats red ones.

Fig. 18-6. Hemp headwear
(Mural on the west wall of the burial chamber,
Deokheung-ri Mural Tomb in Nampo,
North Korea)

Fig. 18-7. Warrior's helmet
(Mural on the western side of the burial
chamber's south wall, Anak Tomb No. 2 in Anak,
North Korea)

Fig. 18-8. Topknot
(Mural on the east wall of the burial chamber,
Yaksu-ri Mural Tomb in Nampo, North Korea)

Fig. 19-1. *Geongwick*
(Mural on the northeast wall of the burial chamber, Gakjeochong in Ji'an, China)

Women wore two types of hairstyles (fig. 19): the up style worn by married women (*ollin meori*) and the ponytail worn by unmarried women and children (*naerin meori*). The up style itself is divided into two types: the first style had the hair wound up on top of the head and was worn by commoners (*eonjeun meori*); and the second had the hair twisted in one or many ring shapes and was worn by the upper classes and royal family members (*goriteun meori*). While excavated feminine ornaments include hairpins called *binyeo*, gold rings and bracelets, Goguryeo murals depict many more types being worn.

Fig. 19-2. *Geongwick*
(Mural on the south wall of the first burial chamber, Samsilchong in Ji'an, China)

Fig. 19-3. *Goriteun meori* hairstyle ↑
(Mural on the north wall of the western side chamber attached to the antechamber, Anak Tomb No. 3 in Anak, North Korea)

Fig. 19-4. *Ollin meori* hairstyle ↗
(Mural on the north wall of the burial chamber, Deokheung-ri Mural Tomb in Nampo, North Korea)

Fig. 19-5. *Naerin meori* hairstyle ↑
(Mural on the northeast wall of the burial chamber, Gakjeochong in Ji'an, China)

Fig. 19-6. *Naerin meori* hairstyle ↗
(Mural on the south wall of the first burial chamber, Samsilchong in Ji'an, China)

Fig. 20-1. Ankle-high leather shoes
(Mural on the north wall of the burial chamber, Suryeopchong in Nampo, North Korea)

Fig. 20-2. White Shoes
(Mural on the north wall of the burial chamber, Deokheung-ri Mural Tomb in Nampo, North Korea)

Fig. 20-3. Shoes with gaiters
(Mural on the west wall of the burial chamber, Susan-ri Mural Tomb in Nampo, North Korea)

Fig. 20-4. Shoes with upturned tips
(Mural on the ceiling corbels of the burial chamber, Ohoebun Tomb No.4 in Ji'an, China)

As for footwear, murals show shoes that reached the ankle as well as lower ones (fig. 20). All shoes featured upturned tips at the toes called *ko*. Goguryeo people also wore socks called *beoseon* that also had upturned tips. Many murals and other relics confirm the existence of combat shoes armored with sharp nails hammered to protrude from the sole.

4 Food, Cuisine, Table Settings

The staple foods of the Goguryeo people were millet, wheat, barley, soybeans and other grains. Burned grains were found in Goguryeo ruins in Ji'an, China. People ground the grains and then cooked them in steamer bowls, evidence for which has been excavated from many Goguryeo sites. For instance, the mural in Anak Tomb No. 3 portrays a woman stirring grains inside a steamer bowl placed on a fire pit (fig. 21).

To supplement their diet, the Goguryeo people raised cows, pigs, chickens, dogs and other livestock and hunted boars, deer, and pheasants. *Maekjeok* (貊炙), similar to today's *bulgogi*, has been confirmed as one of their meat dishes. Records on *Dongyizhuan* (東夷傳) in Chinese historical chronicles state that the Okjeo people in Hamgyeong-do province brought fish and salt to Gungnaeseong of Goguryeo, indicating that seafood was also incorporated into their diet at that time.

Fig. 21-1. Kitchen ↑
(Mural on the east wall of the eastern side chamber attached to the antechamber, Anak Tomb No. 3 in Anak, North Korea)

Fig. 21-2. Earthenware steamer and iron kettle ↗
(Guui-dong Fort in Seoul, Seoul National University Museum)

The kitchens in the residences of aristocrats were separated from the women's quarters. Female servants carried food on trays to the main room in the women's or men's quarters and placed the dishes on the table. The Muyongchong mural shows that individual tables were set for the master of the house and each of his guests (fig. 22).

Fig. 22-1. Delivery of food tables (replica)
(Mural on the southeast wall of the burial chamber, Muyongchong in Ji'an, China)

Fig. 22-2. Setting out food tables for the tomb occupant and his wives (replica)
(Mural on the northeast wall of the burial chamber, Gakjeochong in Ji'an, China)

Plays

5

Many Chinese historical documents mention that the Goguryeo people enjoyed singing, dancing and acrobatic performances. These were often performed at feasts offered by the king and aristocrats or during processions of ceremonial or military music. Acrobatic performances called *nori*, *gyoye* (較藝), *gogye* (曲藝), *giye* (技藝), *hwansul* (幻術) or circuses were presented by troupes, usually during an aristocratic procession or at a residence when guests had been invited. Jangcheon Tomb No. 1 depicts a scene where the master and his guests are enjoying acrobatic performances at a picnic while the Susan-ri Mural Tomb illustrates an aristocratic couple watching performances. The Yaksu-ri Mural Tomb shows professionals performing before a large-scale procession of an aristocrat.

A Goguryeo troupe would perform horse riding, juggling with hands and feet, swordplay and animal taming. The Susan-ri Mural Tomb shows performers wearing jackets with narrow sleeves and tight pants as they juggle with their hands (fig. 23). One juggler opens his knees slightly and keeps them bent, turns his hip back, leans his head back at a right angle, and puts his hands in the air. Above him in the air, he is juggling three poles and five balls, with only one of the balls actually in his hand. The tension in the juggler's hands, eyes and toes is evident as he follows the three-quarter time. Behind him, another performer in similar attire and posture tosses a many-spoked wheel into the air. Above them, a performer holds two small objects while standing on a wooden bridge that is as tall as a man.

The Palcheong-ri Mural Tomb shows an extensive variety of performances except for animal taming (fig. 24). Feasts include horse riding, hand juggling with poles and balls to the accompaniment of a horn trumpet, foot juggling on a high wooden bridge to instrumental accompaniment, and sword duels. As juggling is shown in almost all of the murals, it must have been very popular among the Goguryeo people. We can conclude from the juggling performances depicted in the

Fig. 23. Acrobatics
(Mural on the west
wall of the burial
chamber,
Susan-ri Mural Tomb
in Nampo, North
Korea)

Palcheong-ri Mural Tomb and Susan-ri Mural Tomb that
juggling had reached its peak of popularity in the fifth century.

Fig. 24. Acrobatics (tracing)
(Mural on the east wall of antechamber, Palcheong-ri Mural Tomb in Daedong,
North Korea)

Fig. 25. Acrobatics
(Mural on the north wall of the antechamber, Jangcheon Tomb No.1 in Ji'an,
China)

Jangcheon Tomb No. 1 depicts the aristocrat hosting a picnic at which the troupe performs. A member of the troupe performs a skill called *ganduhui* (竿頭戲) [fig. 25]. He leans his head back, bending his knees and pushing his hip backwards, and is about to throw the ball in his left hand into the air. A ball rests on a small board that sits atop the pole grasped in his right hand and another board is placed atop the first ball, with a second ball set on the top board. The other performer, with knees bent and head thrown back, brandishes a club in his right hand. Sitting on the table next to him is a wheel which might be one of the items for the performance.

Animal taming is illustrated only in Jangcheon Tomb No. 1 where the mural depicts two monkeys climbing up and down a large tree situated between the master and his guest. One yellow monkey climbing down from the tree has his neck bound and wears a white mask. Also on the trunk, another yellow monkey, wearing a white bear's mask, is bowing to the occupant of the tomb sitting on the chair to the right. Utilizing the big tree as both stage and instrument, the monkeys perform before the couple. All of the performers wear short, narrow-sleeved jackets and narrow pants.

6 Dancing and Singing

The Goguryeo people took pleasure in watching dancers wearing long jackets with long sleeves and roomy pants. They liked to see the dancers spin around and flutter their attire while bending and extending their arms. This was a genre of Goguryeo dance and very popular in ancient East Asia. Dance can be categorized into solo, pair and group dances; dance accompanied by instruments or dance without instruments; and dance choruses of men or women. These varieties of dance can be distinguished on the Goguryeo murals.

Dancers and musicians often wore make-up, powdering their faces and applying red lipstick to their lips and red spots called *yeonji* and *gonji* on their foreheads and their cheeks. A scene painted in Jangcheon Tomb No. 1 shows a meeting between a carefully made-up dancer and a pentachord player, as the

Fig. 26. Dancing
(Mural on the north wall of the antechamber, Jangcheon Tomb No. 1 in Ji'an, China)

dancer performs with her long sleeves fluttering smoothly and lightly to the sounds of the pentachord known as *ohyeongeum*

(五鉉琴) (fig.26). In Anak Tomb No. 3, the mural depicts three seated musicians playing the gin *jeo*, *wanham* (阮咸) and the yukhyeon *geomungo* (fig. 27). Unlike other murals, Anak Tomb No. 3 shows a dancer wearing a mask with a high nose bridge. The dancer's movements are very dynamic and reminiscent of the *hoseonmu* (胡旋舞) of West and Central Asia. Of course, her attire is suitable for dynamic movement: her sleeves are short

Fig. 27. Dance with musical accompaniment (tracing)
(Mural on the west wall of the burial chamber, Anak Tomb No. 3 in Anak, North Korea)

Goguryeo

and narrow and the girth of her pants is also narrow. Tonggu Tomb No. 12 depicts two dancers performing with a *geomungo* player (fig. 28). These murals clearly illustrate the unique features and variety of Goguryeo dance.

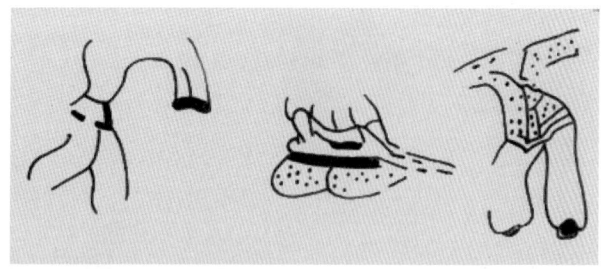

Fig. 28. Dancing (tracing)
(Mural on the west wall of the burial chamber, southern chamber of Tonggu Tomb No. 12 in Ji'an, China)·

In addition to the solo dance described in the previous examples, the Muyongchong mural depicts a group dance that highlights five dancers following a lead dancer and a seven-member chorus (fig. 29). Groups of two or three are arranged in lines, wearing special attire to enhance the impact of the choreography. The two dancers on the right are clad in jackets and pants with reverse color schemes from one another, while two among the three left-hand dancers wear the same long coats with different colors so that the audience can clearly see the harmony of color and movement. Even during the Goguryeo period, much thought was devoted to the style and presentation of the dance.

Fig. 29. Dancing (replica)
(Mural on the southeast wall of the burial chamber, Muyongchong in Ji'an, China)

A large-scale procession painted in Anak Tomb No. 3 draws our attention because a dancer performs with a sword and bow in his hands (fig. 30). The procession portrayed in the Palcheong-ri Mural Tomb also includes a sword performance. Two men hold long swords in their hands while jumping up and down as part of an act for the audience. This type of performance was a combination of play and training. When the dancers performed with weapons, they were accompanied by musical

60

Fig. 30. Dancing
(Corridor mural, eastern side of the burial chamber, Anak Tomb No. 3 in Anak, North Korea)

instruments such as drums, flutes or horns which made loud, piercing sounds. Anak Tomb No. 3 depicts a performance with a drum, one of the oldest versions of the drum performance still extant today. A similar drum performance also appears in Ohoebun Tomb No. 5. This weapon-wielding performer wears a jacket with short sleeves and narrow pants. Some male performers even wore pants with the crotch area securely fastened up high.

7 Musical Instruments

Tomb murals of Goguryeo and historical documents on Goguryeo confirm the existence of 36 different kinds of musical instruments. Musical instruments were divided into stringed, wind and percussion. The *geomungo* with four, five and six strings are representative of the stringed instruments, and three types of *geomungo* have been found depicted on tomb murals (fig. 31). The *geomungo* with six strings in Anak

Fig. 31. *Geomungo*
(Mural on the ceiling corbels of the burial chamber, Muyongchong in Ji'an, China)

Fig. 32-1. *Wanham* ↑
(Mural on the north wall of the antechamber, Deokheung-ri Mural Tomb in Nampo, North Korea)

Fig. 32-2. *Wanham* ↗
(Mural on the ceiling corbels of the first burial chamber, Samsilchong in Ji'an, China)

Tomb No. 3 is similar to the *hyeonhakgeum* (玄鶴琴) described in the *Samguk sagi* (三國史記) and known to be made by Wang, San-ak (王山岳), the greatest musician of Goguryeo. Another stringed instrument, *wanham* (阮咸), has a round sound box and a long neck (fig. 32). According to documents of the period, *wanham* belonged to the same general family as a Chinese lute called *bipa* (琵琶) and was developed and widely used in Central Asia. It often appears in the murals of Anak Tomb No. 3, Samsilchong and Ohoebun Tomb No. 5. As some musicians in the murals resemble Central Asians, it can be surmised that Goguryeo benefited from cultural exchanges with other states in Central Asia.

Fig. 33-1. Horn trumpet →
(Corridor mural, eastern side of
the burial chamber, Anak Tomb
No. 3 in Anak, North Korea)

Fig. 33-2. Horn trumpet ↓
(Mural on the south wall of the
antechamber, Deokheung-ri
Mural Tomb in Nampo, North
Korea)

Fig. 33-3. Horn trumpet
(Mural on the ceiling corbels of the first burial chamber, Samsilchong in Ji'an, China)

As for wind instruments, horn trumpets were used to signal and control the movement of large groups including processions, and were often pictured in the tomb murals (fig. 33). The trumpet was considered an important instrument for the type of processional music known as *gochwiak* (鼓吹樂). Flutes such as *gin jeo*, *jeotdae* and *so* (簫) were preferred as accompaniment for acrobatics and dance performances (fig. 34). *So* was an instrument that very much resembled the modern-day harmonica and was made out of several small pieces of bamboo that were tied together.

Fig. 34. *So*
(Corridor mural, eastern side of the burial chamber, Anak Tomb No. 3 in Anak, North Korea)

In Goguryeo, various types of percussion instruments — including drums, bells and gongs — were used in many different occasions. In particular, drums were an important part of *gochwiak* music. Standing drums, hanging drums, *janggu* (hourglass-shaped drums) and other drums can be seen in the tomb murals (fig. 35). *Janggu*, sometimes called *yogo* (腰鼓), were popular in Central Asia and spread to Goguryeo. Bells and gongs appear in Anak Tomb No. 3 (fig. 36); the gong in the murals is a type of *yo* (鐃) or *jeong* (鉦) used for military marches.

Fig. 35-1. Drum
(Corridor mural, eastern side of the burial chamber, Anak Tomb No. 3 in Anak,
North Korea)

Fig. 35-2. Drum
(Mural on the south wall of the antechamber, Deokheung-ri Mural Tomb in Nampo,
North Korea)

Fig. 35-3. Drum
(Mural on the east wall of the
burial chamber, Susan-ri Mural
Tomb in Nampo, North Korea)

Fig. 35-4. *Janggu* ↓
(Mural on the ceiling corbels
of the burial chamber,
Ohoebun Tomb No. 4 in Ji'an,
China)

Fig. 36. Gongs and bells
(Corridor mural, eastern side of the burial chamber, Anak Tomb No. 3 in Anak, North Korea)

Gochwiak, a processional music, is a type of group performance played by percussion and wind instruments. The development and significance of *gochwiak* in Goguryeo society can be confirmed in murals. The murals of the Pyeongyangyeokjeon Mural Tomb, Anak Tomb No. 3, Gamsinchong, and the Yaksu-ri Mural Tomb all indicate the procession of a *gochwiak* group. Among them, Anak Tomb No. 3 is noteworthy in that it portrays a large-scale processional group on the corridor mural **(fig. 37)**. The group consists of 64 members, divided into *tagodae* (打鼓隊, drums) and *gochwidae* (marching band). They play nine types of percussion instruments including drums, bells and gongs and 28 members play small and big horn trumpets.

Fig. 37. Marching Band
(Corridor mural, eastern side of the burial chamber, Anak Tomb No. 3 in Anak, North Korea)

Sports and Hunting 8

The geographical location of Goguryeo exposed its people to many small and large-scale wars. Thus, athletic exercises had to be both martial and practical in nature and included horse riding, archery, wrestling, and *subak* (手搏). The horse riding and archery called *masahui* depicted in the Deokheung-ri Mural Tomb were skills that were tested in small and large-scale hunting contests and national hunting competitions held in Nangnang (樂浪) valley on the third day of the third lunar month every year (fig. 38). The athletic and hunting prowess of the Goguryeo people was further developed through these contests.

Fig. 38. Archery contest on horseback (*Masahui*)
(Mural on the west wall of the antechamber, Deokheung-ri Mural Tomb in Nampo, North Korea)

Fig. 39-1. Hunting ↑
(Mural on the ceiling corbels of the antechamber, Deokheung-ri Mural Tomb in Nampo, North Korea)

Fig. 39-2. Hunting ↗
(Mural on the west and south walls of the antechamber, Yaksu-ri Mural Tomb in Nampo, North Korea)

Fig. 39-3. Hunting (replica)
(Mural on the northwest wall of the burial chamber, Muyongchong in Ji'an, China)

Fig. 39-4. Hunting with falconry
(Mural on the south wall of the first burial chamber, Samsilchong in Ji'an, China)

Fig. 39-5. Hunting with falconry
(Mural on the north wall of the antechamber, Jangcheon Tomb No.1 in Ji'an, China)

In addition, Korean wrestling called *ssireum* and *subak* competitions, regarded as part of ordinary play, were held at harvest feasts or at the annual national contest called *gukjung daehoe* (國中大會). Hunting scenes are depicted in the Deokheung-ri Mural Tomb, Muyongchong, the Yaksu-ri Mural Tomb, Tonggu Tomb No. 12, indicating that hunting allowed the participants to obtain food and to prepare offerings for rituals. It also provided an opportunity for exercise and training (fig. 39). The murals show that the Goguryeo people caught tigers, boars, deers and pheasants in a variety of ways—hunting on foot with spears, mounted archery, and hunting with falconry. They also show that the people used both beaters and hounds to flush out game. *Ssireum* scenes are painted in the Gakjeochong and Jangcheon Tomb No. 1, *subakhui* scenes can be seen in Anak Tomb No. 3 and Muyongchong (fig. 40).

Fig. 40-1. *Ssireum*
(Mural on the southeast wall of the burial chamber, Gakjeochong in Ji'an, China)

Fig. 40-2. *Ssireum*
(Mural on the north wall of the antechamber, Jangcheon Tomb No.1 in Ji'an, China)

Fig. 40-3. *Subak*
(Mural on the east wall of the antechamber, Anak Tomb No. 3 in Anak, North Korea)

Fig. 40-4. *Subak*
(Mural on the ceiling corbels of the burial
chamber, Muyongchong in Ji'an, China)

Carriages 9

In ancient and medieval societies, carriages were used for transportation. The type and form of carriages used in Goguryeo can be ascertained from the murals (fig. 41). Horse-drawn carriages were reserved for males and ox-drawn carriages for females. However,

Fig. 41-1. Ox-drawn carriage
(Corridor mural, eastern side of the burial chamber, Anak Tomb No. 3 in Anak, North Korea)

as more and more male aristocrats came to use ox-drawn carriages in China, it became increasingly popular in Goguryeo as well for both male and female aristocrats to use only ox-drawn carriages. While carriages for female aristocrats and Buddhist monks had canopies, those without canopies were reserved for male aristocrats. The murals show that some of these carriages were also used to transport goods.

Fig. 41-2. Ox-drawn carriage
(Mural on the east wall of the passage, Deokheung-ri Mural Tomb in Nampo, North Korea)

Fig. 41-3. Ox-drawn carriage
(Mural on the northwest wall of the burial chamber, Muyongchong in Ji'an, China)

Gods 10

Objects of Worship

According to the account of fourth-century Goguryeo contained in the *Sanguozhi* (三國志), a Chinese chronicle of history, the Goguryeo people worshipped sacred beings such as *gwisin* (鬼神), *yeongseong* (靈星) and *sajik* (社稷). *Yeongseong*, originally worshipped to ensure a good harvest, indicated *cheonjeonseong* (天田星), or the constellation thought to rule over grains. Another set of Chinese records, *Beishi* (北史), encompassed the history of fifth-century Goguryeo and included descriptions of other gods such as Buyeosin (夫餘神) and Deunggosin (登高神). It is understood that Buyeosin referred to Yuhwa (柳花), the daughter of Habaek (河伯), as the Earth Mother, while Deunggosin represented Jumong (the founding father of Goguryeo), born of a union between Yuhwa and Haemosu (解慕漱), the Heavenly Emperor's son.

According to the *Jiutangshu* (舊唐書), which addressed the collapse of Goguryeo, new gods such as Ilsin (日神), Gahansin (可汗神), and Gijasin (箕子神) sprang up during this period. Examining the names of the gods, we can assume that Gahansin and Gijasin are the deified heroes Gahan and Gija.

An annual ceremony held in the tenth lunar month honored the god Susin (隧神). Records state that during Dongmaeng (東盟) festival, the annual ritual devoted to Heaven, the Susin was brought from a large cave in the east of Gungnaeseong in order to unite people and resolve conflicts in society. This Susin was presumed to be the Earth Mother, that is, the daughter of Habaek, the water god (水神), who is sometimes thought to be higher than Deunggosin (Jumong).

Tomb murals dating to the sixth century in Ohoebun Tomb No. 4 and Ohoebun Tomb No. 5 in Ji'an, China depict gods of the sun and the moon holding their respective celestial orbs above their heads [fig. 42]. These gods each possess the torso of a man but have a dragon's body below the waist. It seems that the figures of the Chinese gods Fuxi (伏羲) and Nuwa (女媧) were fused with the Goguryeo gods of the sun and the moon. Haemosu, known as the father of Jumong, was considered a sun god and his wife Yuhwa, a moon goddess.

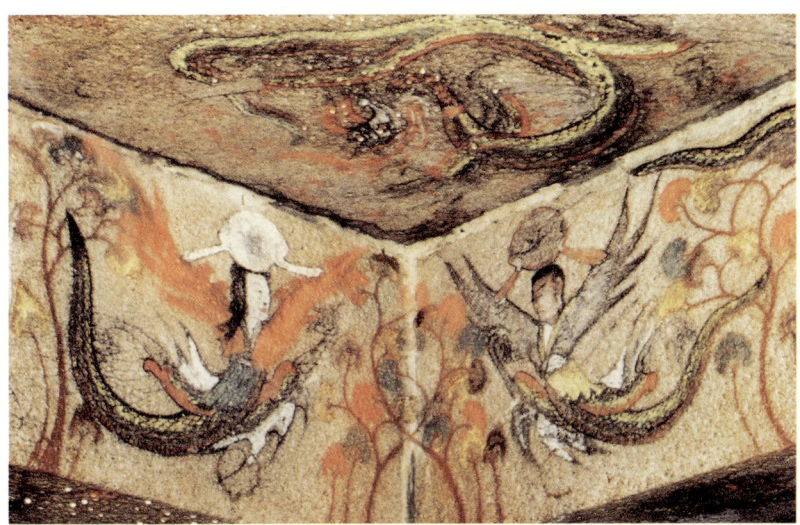

Fig. 42. God of the sun and goddess of the moon
(Mural on the ceiling corbels of the burial chamber, Ohoebun Tomb No. 4 in Jian, China)

This understanding of Haemosu is confirmed by the *Jewang ungi* (帝王韻紀), a chronicle written during the Goryeo (高麗) period (918-1392), which describes "Haemosu riding on a carriage drawn by five dragons claiming himself as a son of the Heavenly Emperor, traveling to the sky and the earth and governing the state (Goguryeo)." Goguryeo people called him Cheonwangnang (天王郎), which indicates that Haemosu was a sun god with the attribute of *yang* (陽). Thus, his wife Yuhwa, a daughter of Habaek, is a goddess of the moon and possesses the attribute of *yin* (陰) of the moon.

In addition to the gods that appear in historical documents, Goguryeo had many gods associated with aspects of civilization; myths and legends related to such gods propagated quickly. In the Ji'an area during the sixth century, the murals show many such gods of civilization including a god of fire, a god of grains, a god of blacksmiths, a god of the wheel and a god of the whetstone (fig. 43). For example, an ox-

Fig. 43. Heaven
(Mural on the ceiling corbels of the burial chamber, Ohoebun Tomb No. 5 in Ji'an, China)

headed, spear-wielding god, described as a god of war in the Samsilchong mural, appears as a god of grains with ears of grain in his hand in the murals during the sixth century (fig. 44). Also painted are a god of fire holding a torch in his right hand, a god of blacksmith striking iron, a god of the wheel manufacturing a newly developed wheel and a god of the whetstone polishing his whetstone (fig. 45)

Fig. 44-1. God of war
(Mural on the ceiling corbels of the second burial chamber, Samsilchong in Ji'an, China)

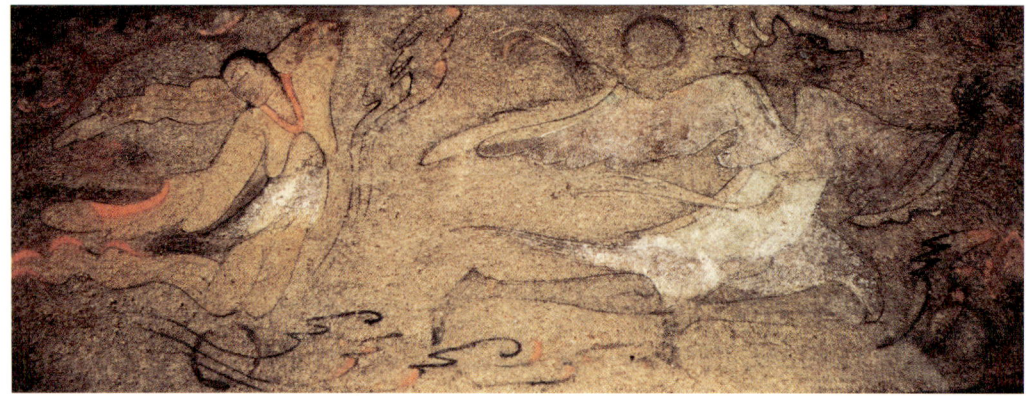

Fig. 44-2. Gods of fire and agriculture
(Mural on the ceiling corbels of the burial chamber, Ohoebun Tomb No. 4 in Ji'an, China)

Fig. 45-1. God of blacksmiths
(Mural on the ceiling corbels of
the burial chamber, Ohoebun
Tomb No. 5 in Ji'an, China)

Fig. 45-2. God of wheel
(Mural on the ceiling corbels of the burial chamber, Ohoebun Tomb No. 4 in Ji'an, China)

Fig. 45-3. God of whetstone
(Mural on the ceiling corbels of the burial chamber, Ohoebun Tomb No. 5 in Ji'an, China)

Fig. 46-1. Immortal
(Mural on the ceiling corbels of the burial chamber, Ohoebun Tomb No. 4 in Ji'an, China)

Fig. 46-2. Immortals
(Mural on the ceiling corbels of the burial chamber, Ohoebun Tomb No. 4 in Ji'an, China)

Fig. 47. Immortal (replica)
(Mural on the ceiling corbels of the burial chamber, Muyongchong in Ji'an, China)

Immortals, Auspicious Animals and Birds

In Goguryeo burial chambers, immortals called *sinseon* (神仙) are drawn on ceilings along with heavenly constellations. They appear to fly without wings in some cases but usually are depicted riding on cranes, phoenixes, dragons, *girin* and other auspicious birds or animals (fig. 46). According to some Taoist documents, *sinseon* wore clothes called *cheonui* (天衣, divine clothes), had long donkey-like ears and non-human features (fig. 47).

Fig. 48. Heaven
(Mural on the ceiling corbels of the antechamber, Deokheung-ri Mural Tomb in Nampo, North Korea)

The notion of sacred birds and animals was rooted in Taoism and the belief in constellations (fig. 48). Among the sacred beings depicted in murals, auspicious birds held the place of greatest honor, evidence of the Goguryeo people's admiration of and unique belief in the power of birds. Birds named *cheonchu* (千秋) and *manse* (萬歲) with human heads are imaginary creatures to which one prays for longevity or a happier afterlife (fig. 49).

Fig. 49-1. Mythical bird *cheonchu*
(Mural on the ceiling corbels of the burial chamber, Muyongchong in Ji'an, China)

Fig. 49-2. Mythical bird *cheonchu*
(Mural on the ceiling corbels of the second burial chamber, Samsilchong in Ji'an, China)

Fig. 49-3. Mythical bird *manse*
(Mural on the ceiling corbels of the antechamber, Deokheung-ri Mural Tomb in Nampo, North Korea)

Other mythological creatures include the *girin* (麒麟), which is described in an ancient Chinese text as "... looking like a deer, with a forehead like a wolf, a tail like an ox, hooves like a horse, and a horn on its head." Many historical records indicate that the people believed that the *girin* appeared only when the universe was working correctly, that is, when society had reached its ideal (fig. 50). The *girin*, a bringer of peace, is often paired with the phoenix. *Bagwi* (博位), *gilli* (吉利), *bugwi* (富貴), and *yeongyang* (零陽) in the Deokheung-ri Mural Tomb

Fig. 50-1. *Girin*
(Mural on the ceiling corbels of the burial chamber, Anak Tomb No. 1 in Anak, North Korea)

are divine animals related to good/ill luck and fortune/ misfortune refered to as *gilyung hwabok*(吉凶禍福). Not surprisingly, people wished for good luck and fortune and eagerly depicted such imaginary beings in the murals **(fig. 51)**. *Seongseong* (猩猩), as described in the *Shanhaijing* (山海經), is an animal with a human head and the power of speech. As it was believed that the *seongseong* enjoyed drinking, people used alcohol as bait. *Byeokdok* (辟毒) is another auspicious animal believed to help prevent poisoning(毒).

Fig. 50-2. *Girin*
(Mural on the ceiling corbels of the burial chamber, Muyongchong in Ji'an, China)

Fig. 50-3. *Girin*
(Mural on the ceiling corbels of the second burial chamber, Samsilchong in Ji'an, China)

Fig. 50-4. *Girin*
(Mural on the ceiling corbels of the burial chamber, Gangseodaemyo in
Pyeongyang, North Korea)

Fig. 51-1. Mythical bird *yangsu*
(Mural on the ceiling corbels of the burial chamber, Deokheung-ri Mural Tomb in
Nampo, North Korea)

93

Fig. 51-2. Mythical bird
(Mural on the ceiling corbels of the burial chamber, Gangseodaemyo in Pyeongyang, North Korea)

Fig. 51-3. Man-headed animal
(Mural on the ceiling corbels of the burial chamber, Anak Tomb No. 1 in Anak, North Korea)

Fig. 51-4. Heavenly deer *cheollok*
(Mural on the ceiling corbels of the second burial chamber, Samsilchong in Ji'an, China)

Fig. 51-5. Heavenly horse *cheonma*
(Mural on the ceiling corbels of the burial chamber, Deokheung-ri Mural Tomb in Nampo, North Korea)

Fig. 51-6. Mythical flying fish *bieo*
(Mural on the ceiling corbels of the antechamber, Deokheung-ri Mural Tomb in Nampo, North Korea)

Fig. 51-7. Heavenly horse cheonma and mythical flying fish bieo
(Mural on the ceiling corbels of the burial chamber, Anak Tomb No. 1 in Anak, North Korea)

Buddhist Culture 11

In 372, during the reign of King Sosurim (小獸林王), Goguryeo embraced Buddhism as its national religion. That year, the Chinese monk Shundao (順道) was dispatched by Fu Jian (符堅), the king of Former Qin (前秦), to King Sosurim along with Buddhist statues and scriptures (sutra). King Sosurim sanctioned Goguryeo people's belief in Buddhism and the active dissemination of the religion. However, the Goguryeo people in fact had begun to accept Buddhism long before 372. In the early fourth century, Tanshi (曇始), an old monk from Jin (晋) China, arrived in Liaodong to spread Buddhism. Anak Tomb No. 3, constructed in 357, includes a lotus pattern in its murals. In addition, in the mid-fourth century, according to certain records, a venerable monk from Eastern Jin (東晉) was said to have sent a letter to a Goguryeo ascetic.

Fig. 52. Procession for worship to Buddha
(Mural on the west wall of the burial chamber, Ssangyeongchong in Nampo, North Korea)

Goguryeo adopted Buddhism as a national ideology in order to unify the entire society. After the acceptance of Buddhism, many Chinese monks including the monk Adao (阿道) from Eastern Jin entered the kingdom, and new temples were erected all over Goguryeo lands (fig. 52). King Gogugyang (故國壤王), who succeeded King Sosurim, instructed his people to believe in Buddhism in order to obtain blessings (fig. 53). During his reign, King Gwanggaeto the Great (廣開土大王) built nine temples in Pyeongyang alone.

Fig. 53-1. Rites offered before a statue of Buddha
(Mural on the ceiling corbels of the antechamber, Jangcheon Tomb No. 1 in Ji'an, China)

Fig. 53-2. *Bodhisattvas and apsaras*
(Mural on the ceiling corbels of the antechamber, Jangcheon Tomb No. 1 in Ji'an, China)

Fig. 53-3. *Sanhwa gongyang*
(Mural on the ceiling corbels of the burial chamber, Anak Tomb No. 2 in Anak, North Korea)

With the official support of the state, Buddhism influenced the people's notion of the afterlife. According to Buddhism, the afterlife is decided by one's karma. The next life can be lived either in one of the six realms (六道) or can take place in the Buddhist paradise called *jeongto* (淨土), the Pure Land. Before the introduction of Buddhism, most Goguryeo people believed that they would return to spiritual world of their ancestors after they died. However, after Buddhism was introduced, they wished to either go to the world of Buddha or be reborn in the Buddhist paradise. The previous understanding of an afterlife gave way to a new but widely accepted notion of reincarnation and rebirth in the Buddhist paradise. By the fifth century, some of the Goguryeo murals utilized a lotus flower theme, a motif closely related to the recently embraced notion of Buddhism (fig. 54).

After King Jangsu(長壽王) moved the capital to Pyeongyang in 427, Buddhism flourished across the kingdom. The nine-storied pagoda of the Geumgangsa temple(金剛寺塔) in Pyeongyang is a 60-meter wooden tower that stands as a striking example of the people's devotion to Buddhism. It also represents a typical pagoda of the Three Kingdoms period along with Silla Hwangnyongsa pagoda (皇龍寺塔) in Gyeongju and Baekje Mireuksa pagoda(彌勒寺塔) in Iksan.

Fig. 54-1. Ceiling filled with lotuses ↓
(Mural on the ceiling corbels of the burial chamber, Anak Tomb No. 2 in Anak, North Korea)

Fig. 54-2. Lotus, the sun and the moon ↘
(Mural on the ceiling corbels of the burial chamber, Ssangyeongchong in Nampo, North Korea)

Buddhism started to wane, however, during the sixth century. Political controversy over royal succession caused the state to decrease its support of Buddhism. As a result, famous monks like Hyeryang (惠亮) sought asylum in Silla and the social influence of Buddhism gradually weakened. This faltering religion was replaced with Shamanism and Taoism, and in the seventh century, the Odumigyo (五斗米敎), a branch of Taoism gained many adherents. This process of Goguryeo importing and accepting Taoism from Tang China (唐) is reflected in tomb murals painted in the sixth to seventh centuries.

Lotus Flowers and Birth by Transformation 12

Lotus flowers, which possessed great significance in Egypt, India and China long before Buddhism was established in Goguryeo, were used as ornamentation on architecture, objects and clothes. In Egypt, the water lily was recognized as a source of life and rebirth like the sun. In India, the lotus flower was also considered a source of life, with the *Vedas* depicting several gods and animals singing in admiration of the lotus flower. In contrast, in China, while the lotus flower symbolized the sun or the Heavenly Emperor, it was not considered a source of life. It is only after the importation of Buddhism that the Chinese began to link the lotus flower with the creation of life.

Indian Buddhism accepted the Hindu concept of the lotus flower as a symbol of light and life. Like *Vishnu*, the God of Light, who gave birth to *Brahma*, the God of Creation, the

Buddha was considered as a being that emitted the infinite light and this light was expressed as a lotus flower. That is, Buddhism recognized the lotus flower as a basic device and a source of light, life and creation in the world.

Fig. 55. Lotus in the ceiling stone
(Mural on the ceiling corbels of the burial chamber, Anak Tomb No. 3 in Anak, North Korea)

The lotus flower started appearing in murals beginning from the fourth century (fig. 55). By the fifth century, burial chambers featured a variety of lotus flowers. Tomb murals in the Pyeongyang region portray only rough sketches of the flower, while Ji'an murals show the actual details of the flower. These regional differences diminished in the Ssangyeongchong of Goguryeo at the end of the fifth century. As honeysuckle and lotus flower patterns became widespread in the sixth century (fig. 56), paintings in the two areas grew to share more similarities than in the previous century.

In traditional Buddhist thought, *hwasaeng*, or birth by transformation, refers to one of the four ways of birth: birth from an egg (卵生), birth from a womb (胎生), birth from moisture (濕生) and birth by transformation (化生). Buddhism established a new notion that united the lotus flower with a birth by transformation. To Buddhists, to be born from a lotus flower signified escape from the life of the six samsaric destinies through rebirth into the Buddhist paradise, or the Pure Land. This particular concept of the lotus flower depicted in Goguryeo murals indicates that the Goguryeo people accepted this thought (fig. 57). Jangcheon Tomb No. 1 illustrates a boy and a girl being born out of a lotus flower.

Fig. 56-1. Lotus
(Mural on the ceiling corbels of the burial chamber, Jinpa-ri Tomb No. 4 in Pyeongyang, North Korea)

Fig. 56-2. Birth from a lotus flower
(Mural on the north wall of the burial chamber, Jinpa-ri Tomb No. 1 in Pyeongyang, North Korea)

Fig. 57-1. Birth from a lotus flower
(Mural on the ceiling corbels of the burial chamber, Muyongchong in Ji'an, China)

Fig. 57-2. Birth from a lotus flower ↓
(Mural on the ceiling corbels of the second burial chamber, Samsilchong in Ji'an, China)

Fig. 57-3. Birth from a lotus flower
(Mural on the ceiling corbels of the second burial chamber, Samsilchong in Ji'an, China)

Fig. 57-4. Birth from a lotus flower
(Mural on the ceiling corbels of the antechamber, Jangcheon Tomb No. 1 in Ji'an, China)

Fig. 57-5. Birth from a lotus flower ↑
(Mural on the north wall of the burial chamber, Jinpa-ri Tomb No. 1 in Pyeongyang, North Korea)

Fig. 57-6. Lotus pond ←
(Mural on the southern part of the east wall of the entrance passage, Jinpa-ri Tomb No. 4 in Pyeongyang, North Korea)

Fig. 58. A jewel born from lotus
(Mural on the ceiling corbels of the burial chamber, Gangseodaemyo in Nampo, North Korea)

Boju (寶珠), a jewel, is a symbol of piety and supernatural power, which offers an escape from present-day agony and pain endured by sentient beings. A *cintamani*, a jewel that originated in the brain of the Dragon King, cannot be damaged or burned even if placed in a fire. The *boju* drawn in Jangcheon Tomb No. 1, Jinpa-ri Tomb No. 1 and the Gangseodaemyo are surrounded by fire or being born from lotus flowers (fig. 58). *Boju* being born from lotus flowers is one of the most popular themes in Buddhist stone cave temples in China.

Belief in *Yin-Yang*, the Five Elements and Four Directional Deities

13

The *yin-yang* (陰陽) theory holds that all phenomena consist of two opposite aspects, *yin* and *yang*, and that the movements of and changes in *yin* and *yang* give impetus to the development of all things. In other words, the balance between *yin* and *yang* is at the center of humankind and nature. The theory of five elements (五行) explains the interactions and relationships created in phenomena that consist of fire, water, wood, metal and earth and lead to life, death, change and rebirth. These two theories were combined during the Spring and Autumn (春秋, Chunqiu) period in China and developed into a comprehensive and logical view of the cosmos that could be applied to each field of human society. During the Chinese Han Dynasty, every activity from private life to public affairs was subject to this combined theory.

Goguryeo people were well aware of this combined theory from its inception. For that reason, the state aptly utilized the theory of Five Elements when establishing political ideologies, revising political structures, and implementing foreign policies such as in its diplomatic conflicts with Buyeo. Using the theory as a foundation, Goguryeo accepted morality-focused politics and interpreted the causes of natural disasters based on the notion of "man and Heaven affecting and responding to each other." The theory of Five Elements was used to establish and spread the belief in Jumong, the founder of Goguryeo, and to reorganize the kingdom's defense system. Tomb murals of the Four Directional Deities (四神圖), which guard the four cardinal directions can be considered an expression of the Five Elements theory which was popular in Goguryeo at that time.

The Four Directional Deities were imaginary beings represented by Cheongnyong (Blue Dragon), Baekho (White Tiger), Jujak (Red Phoenix), and Hyeonmu (Black Tortoise-Serpent). Each indicated one of the cardinal directions: Blue Dragon, the east; White Tiger, the west; Red Phoenix, the south; and Black Tortoise-Serpent, the north. They were also associated with the four seasons and the 28 constellations (fig. 59). The Four Directional Deities were an independent motif in

Fig. 59-1. Constellations
(Mural on the ceiling stone of the burial chamber, Jinpa-ri Tomb No. 4 in Pyeongyang, North Korea)

Goguryeo murals from the very foundation of the kingdom and one of many themes depicted on the ceilings of main chambers in the early period. Later they evolved to become the predominant theme. During the early period, the Four

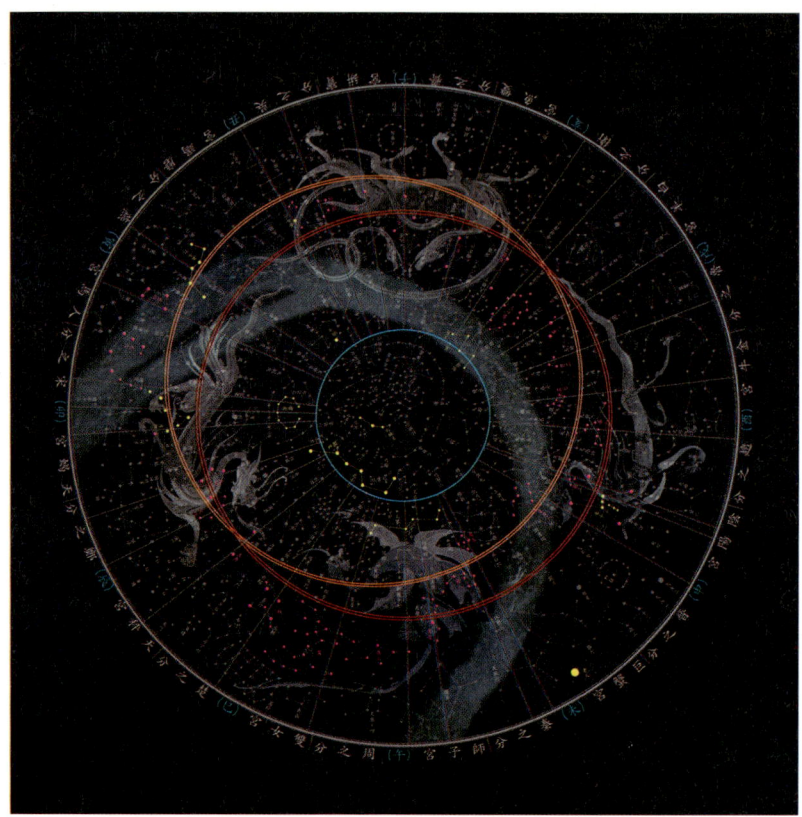

Fig. 59-2. Four Directional Deities and the 28 constellations
(Kim, Il-kwon)

Directional Dieties were relatively unimportant subject in the murals, and were painted as a pair with awkwardly ill-proportioned and imbalanced features (fig. 60).

Fig. 60-1. Cheongnyong (Blue Dragon)
(Mural on the east wall of the burial chamber, Yaksu-ri Mural Tomb in Nampo, North Korea)

Fig. 60-2. Baekho (White Tiger)
(Mural on the west wall of the burial chamber, Yaksu-ri Mural Tomb in Nampo, North Korea)

Fig. 60-3. Jujak (Red Phoenix)
(Mural on the south wall of the burial chamber, Yaksu-ri Mural Tomb in Nampo, North Korea)

Fig. 60-4. Hyeonmu (Black Tortoise-Serpent)
(Mural on the north wall of the burial chamber, Yaksu-ri Mural Tomb in Nampo, North Korea)

In later Goguryeo murals, Blue Dragon and White Tiger were drawn individually, while Red Phoenix was pictured in pairs and Black Tortoise-Serpent as a cross between a tortoise and serpent (fig. 61). Blue Dragon and White Tiger were considered spiritual animals that drove away evil spirits, while Red Phoenix and Black Tortoise-Serpent were seen as divine animals that harmonized *yin* and *yang*.

Four Directional Deities in the later Goguryeo murals were situated on each wall as defenders and guardians of the tomb's occupant. In contrast to Goguryeo murals, Chinese murals in Southern and Northern Dynasties, Sui and Tang depicted the Four Directional Deities only on the ceilings of the main chambers, not on the walls. The different placement and importance given to the deities reveal that Goguryeo and China had divergent perceptions of the Four Directional Dieties.

Fig. 61-1. Cheongnyong
(Mural on the east wall of
the burial chamber, Honam-
ri Sasinchong in
Pyeongyang, North Korea)

Fig. 61-2. Cheongnyong
(Mural on the east wall of the burial chamber, Gangseodaemyo in Nampo, North Korea)

Fig.61-3. Baekho
(Mural on the west wall of
the burial chamber,
Honam-ri Sasinchong in
Pyeongyang, North Korea)

Fig. 61-4. Baekho
(Mural on the west wall of
the burial chamber,
Gangseodaemyo in Nampo,
North Korea)

Fig. 61-5, 6. Jujak
(Mural on the south wall of the burial chamber, Honam-ri Sasinchong in Pyeongyang, North Korea)

Fig. 61-7, 8. Jujak
(Mural on the south wall of the burial chamber, Gangseodaemyo in Nampo, North Korea)

Fig. 61-9. Hyeonmu
(Mural on the north wall of the burial chamber, Honam-ri Sasinchong in Pyeongyang, North Korea)

Fig. 61-10. Hyeonmu
(Mural on the north wall of the burial chamber, Gangseodaemyo in Nampo, North Korea)

Fig. 61-11. Hwangnyong (Yellow Dragon)
(Mural on the ceiling stone of the burial chamber,
Gangseodaemyo in Nampo, North Korea)

Sun, Moon and Constellations 14

Sun and Moon

As Jumong was considered to be son of the sun and the moon and as a grandchild of Habaek, the sun and the moon symbolized the national identity of Goguryeo. Thus, every Goguryeo mural contains the sun and the moon, with the sun depicted as a three-legged crow inside a wheel and the moon represented as one or two toads, rabbits or cinnamon trees inside a wheel (fig. 62). In most cases, the crow with a peacock crest is depicted in flight but in some cases a pigeon or wild goose appears instead. Toads in the wheel appear to lie on their stomachs but in other paintings emit fire and look like golden beetles. Rabbits in the moon grind herbs of immortality in a mortar or simply stand motionless. The placement of the sun and the moon on the ceiling indicates the east and the west, respectively.

Fig. 62-1. Sun and moon
(Mural on the ceiling stone of the burial chamber, Jinpa-ri Tomb No. 1 in Nampo, North Korea)

Fig. 62-2. Sun
(Mural on the ceiling corbels of the burial chamber, Gakjeochong in Ji'an, China)

Fig. 62-3. Sun ↑
(Mural on the ceiling corbels of the burial chamber, Ssangyeongchong in Nampo, North Korea)

Fig. 62-4. Sun ↗
(Mural on the ceiling corbels of the burial chamber, Ohoebun Tomb No. 4 in Ji'an, China)

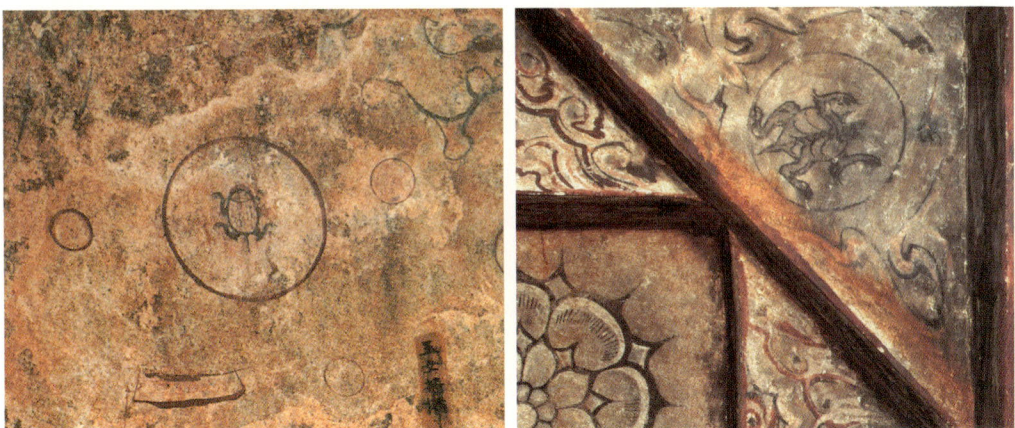

Fig. 62-5. Moon ↑
(Mural on the ceiling corbels of the antechamber, Deokheung-ri Mural Tomb in Nampo, North Korea)

Fig. 62-6. Moon ↗
(Mural on the ceiling corbels of the burial chamber, Ssangyeongchong in Nampo, North Korea)

Fig. 62-7. Moon
(Mural on the ceiling corbels of the burial chamber, Deokhwa-ri Tomb No. 1 in Daedong, North Korea)

Big Dipper and Other Constellations

The ceilings of the burial chamber are adorned with the sun, the moon and other constellations, evidence that the Goguryeo people believed in the power of constellations to influence their lives. The Big Dipper and the Archer were often painted along with the sun and the moon. While the sun and the moon indicate the east and the west, the "Namdu Six Stars (南斗六星)" found in the Archer Constellation and the Big Dipper(北斗七星)

Fig. 63. Sun, moon, Big Dipper ↑
(Mural on the ceiling corbels of the burial chamber, Jangcheon Tomb No. 1
in Ji'an, China)

Fig. 64. Big Dipper ↗
(Mural on the ceiling corbels of the burial chamber, Deokhwa-ri Tomb No. 1
in Daedong, North Korea)

represent the south and the north. During the Wei and Jin periods in China, Taoism assigned great importance to these north and south constellations, asserting that "the Namdu Six Stars controls life while the Big Dipper controls death." It is highly possible that Goguryeo people held a similar belief in these constellations. The Big Dipper was found on the ceiling of the main chamber in Jangcheon Tomb No. 1 along with the

Fig. 65. Big Dipper and earth axis
(Mural on the ceiling corbels of the antechamber, Deokheung-ri Mural Tomb in Nampo, North Korea)

sun and the moon (fig. 63). In addition, the characters "北斗七青" are written in red next to the constellation. Deokhwa-ri Tomb No. 1 and Deokhwa-ri Tomb No. 2 show a Big Dipper that is larger and clearer than any other constellations (fig. 64), demonstrating how deeply the Goguryeo people venerated this constellation (fig. 65).

Tombs 15

In the area of Ji'an alone, more than 13,000 Goguryeo tombs have been found but the majority had been severely damaged (fig. 66). As a result, the internal structure and facilities of those tombs could not be closely analyzed. Basic examination revealed that the stone mound tomb developed into the stone chamber tomb. The early style of the stone mound tomb lacked a

Fig. 66-1. Sanseongha Tombs in Ji'an, China

Fig. 66-2. Cheonchuchong in Ji'an, China

Fig. 66-3. Jechong of Sanseongha Tombs in Ji'an, China

Fig. 67-1. Janggunchong in Ji'an, China(1920s)   Fig. 67-2. Janggunchong in Ji'an, China(2007)

stylobate, or platform, which only began to appear later on. The Janggunchong in Ji'an, an example of the most developed style of a stone mound tomb, is a step pyramid-type stone mound tomb with a stone chamber (fig. 67). The stone chamber tomb can be categorized into a multi-chamber tomb and a single chamber tomb according to the number of chambers (fig. 68). There are also various styles of stone chamber tombs according to the structure of the ceiling corbels: *saasik* (四阿式), *kkeokkeumsik* (折天井式, vaulted corbels), *gungnyungsik* (窮隆式, curved corbels), *pyeonghaeng goimsik* (平行支送式, parallel corbels) and *samgak goimsik* (三角支送 式, triangle corbels) styles. The Gangseodaemyo and the Gangseojungmyo are forms of stone chamber tombs which have

Fig. 68-1. Anak Tomb No. 3 in Anak, North Korea

Fig. 68-2. The interior of Anak Tomb No. 3 in Anak, North Korea

Fig. 68-3. Janggun Tomb of Michanggu Tombs in Huanren, China

Fig. 68-4. The interior of Janggun Tomb of Michanggu Tombs in Huanren (replica)

(Liaoning Province Museum, China)

Fig. 68-5. Mausoleum of King Dongmyeong the Great in Pyeongyang, North Korea

single chambers and *samgak goimsik* ceilings (fig. 69). Murals appear throughout the development of the stone chamber tombs. Early tomb murals did not have a standardized form. Some tombs had corridors, multi-coffin chambers, and included small niches called *gam* (龕) separated from the murals on the right- and left-hand sides of the main chamber. Other tombs had entrance passages running along one side or in the middle of the walls of the burial chamber. In Taeseong-ri Tomb No. 3, a separate passage was constructed at one end of the corridor

Fig. 69-1. Gangseodaemyo in Nampo, North Korea

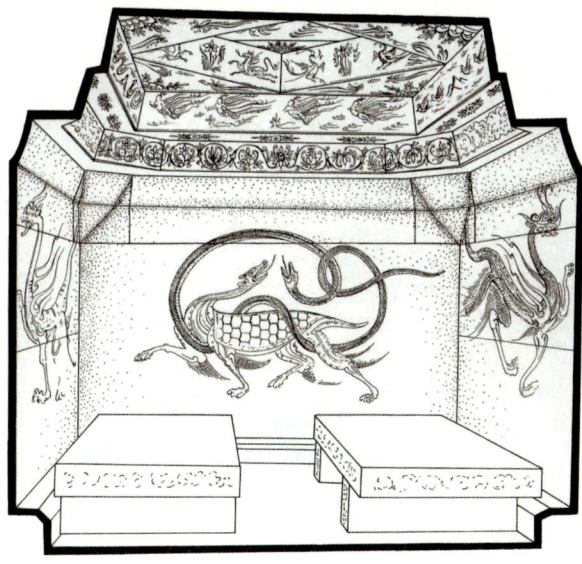

Fig. 69-2. Perspective view of
the interior of Gangseodaemyo
in Nampo, North Korea

Fig. 70. Passage of Taeseong-ri Tomb No. 3 in Nampo, North Korea

surrounding the main chamber, which is very unusual (fig. 70). The structure of the ceiling in the tombs varied: *samgak goimsik*, *kkeokeumsik*, *gungnyungsik*, and *pyeonghaeng goimsik* styles. More than two styles were used in combination or some cases used flat ceilings.

Unlike early mural tombs in which the type of tomb structure is difficult to distinguish, mid-period mural tombs can be largely divided into two-chamber and single-chamber tombs. Simplification into a single-chamber tomb type was difficult due to the significance of various life customs incorporated into the murals. Basically, the two-chamber tomb belongs to the multi-chamber tomb. The Deokheung-ri Mural Tomb represents a typical type of two-chamber tomb, while Gakjeochong demonstrates how the antechamber gradually disappeared (fig. 71).

Between the late fifth century and the early sixth century, a period of further development in mural tombs, the typical single-chamber tomb, in which the entrance passage was situated in the middle of the entrance to the square-shaped main chamber, was most common (fig. 72). These mural tombs were characterized by Four Directional Deities, exhibited a standardized ceiling style. In most cases, the main chamber's ceiling featured *pyeonghaeng samgak goimsik* or *samgak goimsik* style.

The construction method of mural tombs (usually stone-chamber tombs) varied depending on the era and the size of the tomb

Fig. 71-1. Floor plan of the understructure of the Deokheung-ri Mural Tomb in Nampo, North Korea ↑

Fig. 71-2. Floor plan of the understructure of Gakjeochong in Ji'an, China ↗

itself. In the case of a large stone chamber tomb, pebbles found in the river were spread around the tomb to demarcate its boundary. However, except in a few cases, many details including the width and size of the boundary have not been identified. Most grave mounds are rectangular, in line with the traditional stone tombs of Goguryeo. When building up the mound, lime was mixed into the soil or a mass of lime was put into the soil. This helped to sustain the mound and preserve the mural in the burial chamber. Mixing the soil with pebbles

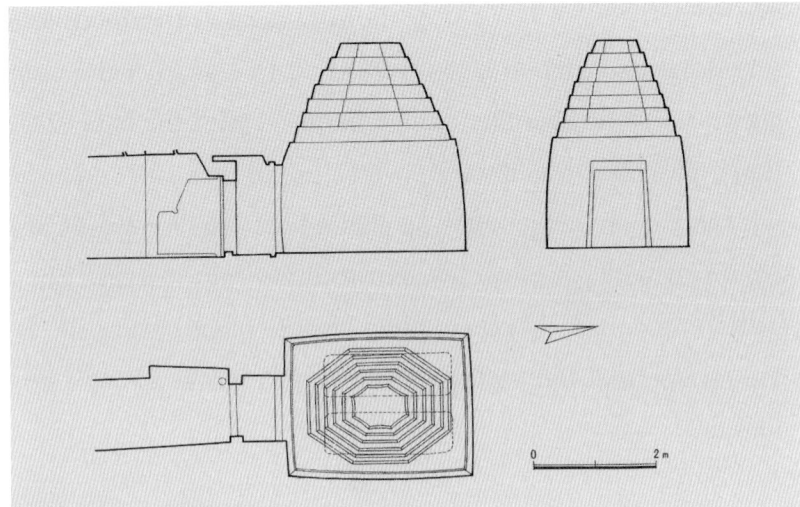

Fig. 72. Floor plan of the understructure of Deokhwa-ri Tomb No. 1 in Daedong, North Korea

and covering the mound with pebbles and roof tiles protected the soil mound as well as prevented moisture and rain from seeping into the tomb. For the same purpose, clay was mixed with lime and charcoal as a sealant after the gap between the large stone slabs was closed with small pebbles outside of the tomb.

In the early and middle periods, the wall and the ceiling of the tomb were finished with lime mortar to close the gaps between the brick-sized stones. After the mid-period, trimmed large limestone and granite slabs were used to construct the more capacious stone chamber tombs. In most cases, the base of the burial chamber was covered with lime mortar and cemented with soil, charcoal, pebbles, sand and lime. The tomb was also equipped with a sewage system to drain rain residue. There was a space made of one to three biers to place coffins on. By the mid-period, the coffin table was also plastered with lime mortar.

As for the multi-chamber tomb of the early and middle periods, a stone pillar was erected at the entrance or around the main chamber to separate other chambers from the main one. In the case of the two-chamber tomb, the builders constructed biers for two coffins at both ends of the main room, a stone pillar in the center of the chamber, and stone figures in the main room (fig. 73). In this case, the stone pillar supported the ceiling of the main chamber.

In addition to the burial chamber, a stone table for religious service was affixed to the inside wall of the antechamber or placed in the main chamber. At one side of the main chamber, a stone coffin bier was installed, while at the other end, a

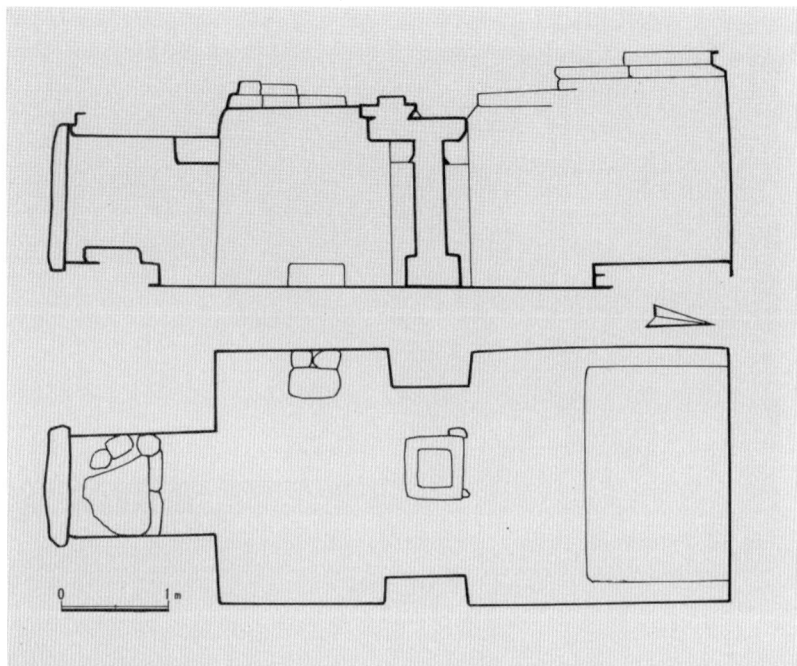

Fig. 73. Floor plan of the understructure of Maseongu Tomb No. 1 in Ji'an, China

traditional fireplace was built and plastered with lime mortar (fig. 74). A single or double stone door closed the entrance to the burial chamber. Typically the entrance passage was made of lime mortar and pebbles, and the inside of the entrance passage was again covered with thick granite slabs.

Fig. 74. Traditional fireplace plastered with lime mortar
(Maseongu Tomb No. 1 in Ji'an, China)

Fortress 16

Relics and tomb murals indicate the basic form and structure of such Goguryeo architectural structures as fortresses, temples, residences and tombs. The Onyeo Mountain Fortress (五女山城) in Huanren (桓仁) is famous for the kingdom's founding myth. Hwando Mountain Fortress (丸都山城) in Ji'an, China and Daeseong Mountain Fortress (大城山城) in Pyeongyang, North Korea are located in the mountains because Goguryeo kings had used the mountains as an important component of the defense infrastructure [fig. 75]. In the seventh century during Yeon Gaesomun's (淵蓋蘇文) rule, Goguryeo built the Cheolli Jangseong Wall (千里長城) in the Liaodong region to protect itself from China. The wall was considered a major component of the state's military defense system. The capital fortresses that remain today include one in Gungnaeseong (國內城) in Ji'an and one in Janganseong (長安城) in Pyeongyang [fig. 76].

Fig. 75-1. Onyeo Mountain Fortress in Huanren, China

Fig. 75-2. Hwando Mountain Fortress in Ji'an, China

Fig. 75-3. Daeseong Mountain Fortress in Pyeongyang, North Korea

Fig. 76-1. Gungnaeseong Fortress in Ji'an, China

Fig. 76-2. Pyeongyangseong Fortress in Pyeongyang, North Korea

To defend itself against the rising colonies of the Chinese Han Dynasty and Buyeo（夫餘）, Goguryeo established a combined defense system in which fortresses were built both in mountains and on flat terrain. Kings, aristocrats and the common people went about their daily lives inside Gungnaeseong fortress, located on flat terrain. In the case of invasion, however, they moved to an emergency fortress like Hwando Mountain Fortress and fended off enemy attacks.

Three types of fortresses were used in the Three Kingdoms period: *temoe*, *pogok* and a combination type. The *temoe* type was constructed along seven- or eight-tenths of the mountain ridges so that the fortress surrounded the mountain top, for example, Onyeo Mountain Fortress in Huanren. This fortress type can be further subdivided into those that surround a mountain peak; those that surround a flat peak; those that surround two nearby mountain tops; those that surround one mountain peak and the ridge of one side of a mountain; and those that surround a lower hill located in flat terrain. The *temoe* type was useful for defense but vulnerable to long-term sieges.

The second type, *pogok* type, included more than one valley in the middle of the fortress, encompassing flat terrain at the bottom and ridges along the side. Due to the uneven topography, the base was not level but the fortress size was large because it contained a valley and flat terrain. Thus, by leveraging the large area and the water in the valley, a reservoir could be created, allowing a greater number of people to stay in the fortress and wage strikes against the enemy on a long-term basis.

The third type, the combination type, combined both of the methods described above, in order to utilize the advantages of both. The combination-type fortresses, which were annexed to older fortresses built in the first or second type, can be found in some areas. Examples of these newer fortresses, constructed by connecting various types of fortresses built in different periods, have been often confirmed.

Fortresses can also be categorized into earthen or stone fortresses, according to their construction materials. In the Three Kingdoms Period, there were many cases where earthen fortresses were partially reinforced by stone materials. Stone fortresses used long pedestal stones called *jangdaeseok*(長臺石) or natural stones so that the wall had a vertical or bow shape. This is in contrast to the earthen fortress that used the geography and natural resources of the surrounding area in construction.

Earthen fortresses were built according to three methods. The first is *saktobeop* (朔土法), which smoothed out steep valley slopes to build the fortress and was often employed when constructing the *temoe*-type fortresses. The second method, *seongtobeop* (成土法), required earth to be dug from inside and outside of the fortress frame and then piled into the center of the frame to build the fortress. When this method was applied,

Fig. 77. *Chi* of Baegamseong Fortress in Dungta, China

Fig. 78. Headquarters of Baegamseong Fortress in Dungta, China

Fig. 79. Secret gate of Pyeongyangseong Fortress in Pyeongyang, North Korea

the hollowed out portion served as a moat. This method was used in the construction of the *temoe*-type fortress as well. Finally, the *panchukbeop* method（板築法）piled up layers of earth to construct the fortress. Usually, clay soil and sandy soil were alternated and at certain sections, a wooden panel called *hyeoppan*（挾板）was fixed to a support to reinforce the fortress wall.

Fig. 80-1. Chart of Yodongseong Fortress (tracing) ⬉
(Mural on the south wall of the antechamber, Yodongseongchong in Suncheon, North Korea)

Fig. 80-2. Fortress chart (tracing) ⬈
(Mural on the south wall of the antechamber, Yonggangdaemyo in Nampo, North Korea)

Fig. 81. Fortress Stone from Pyeongyangseong Fortress in Pyeongyang, North Korea

For defense, every fortress employed its own defensive facilities. Some fortresses included semi-circular, two-layer walled enclosures called *ongseong* (甕城) to protect the main gate and bastions called *chi* (雉) which protruded from the fortress wall to prevent enemies from approaching (fig. 77). Many had furrows filled with water to serve as defensive moats. All fortresses had command posts called *jangdae* (將臺) from which the general commanded his army or for observation of the inside and outside of the fortress (fig. 78). Secret gates called *ammun* (暗門) were also built into fortress walls and hidden from enemy view (fig. 79). These gates were used to transport weapons or food from the outside, dispatch messengers to seek alliances with friendly forces, or to launch raids against the enemy. Fortresses also had floodgates that were used as a sewage system. The Yaksu-ri Mural Tomb, the Yodongseongchong, and the Yonggangdaemyo show in great detail the symmetrical gates, two-story watch towers and internal structures of fortresses of this period (fig. 80). Whenever a new fortress was built, the state appointed one person to be responsible for each section, which is why names are inscribed on each stone of Janganseong in Pyeongyang (fig. 81).

Wars: Weapons, Armor, Battles 17

Weapons

In Chinese records, the Korean people have often been called "people with in the East known for its skill in archery." The Goguryeo people particularly excelled at archery; we see evidence of this in the name of Goguryeo's founding father, Jumong（朱蒙）, which means "skilled archer." Goguryeo was renowned for a specific bow called *maekgung*（貊弓）that was extremely crooked, short and strong **(fig. 82)**. This short bow made of ox horn was smaller than half the height of an average person and very suitable for use on horseback. Goguryeo people also used various types of arrowheads. One type had an axe blade and a flat head to increase impact; another was called a

Fig. 82-1. Archer
(Corridor mural, eastern side of the burial chamber, Anak Tomb No. 3 in Anak, North Korea)

Fig. 82-2. Hunter
(Mural on the northwest wall of the burial chamber, Muyongchong in Ji'an, China)

myeongjeok (crying arrow) in which a cylindrical implement drilled with holes was attached to the middle of the arrowhead to make a whistling sound after being released from the bow. This arrow is seen in the hunting scenes of tomb murals.

Fig. 83-1. Warrior with spear
(Corridor mural, eastern side of the burial chamber, Anak Tomb No. 3 in Anak, North Korea)

Spears, swords and battle-axes were basic weapons used for close combat (fig. 83). The edge of the spear was usually cone-shaped or flat. A hook-shaped spear was also used to snatch the enemy. There were two types of swords: a one-meter long sword and a 30-centimeter short sword. Both had blades on one side and rings on the bottom of their handles. The rings indicated the status of the user, with three types of rings:

Fig. 83-2. Warrior with spear
(Mural on the south wall of the burial chamber,
Anak Tomb No. 2 in Anak, North Korea)

Fig. 83-3. Spear
(Guui-dong Fort in Seoul, Seoul National
University Museum)

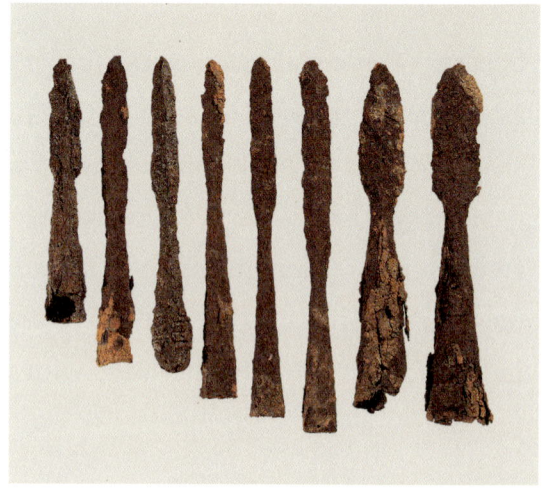

Fig. 83-4. Warrior with sword ↑
(Corridor mural, eastern side of
the burial chamber, Anak Tomb
No. 3 in Anak, North Korea)

Fig. 83-5. Warrior with sword ↖
(Mural on the west wall of the
second burial chamber,
Samsilchong in Ji'an, China)

Fig. 83-6. Sword
(Guui-dong Fort in Seoul, Seoul National University Museum)

Fig. 83-7. Battle-ax warriors
(Corridor mural, eastern side of the burial chamber, Anak Tomb No. 3 in Anak, North Korea)

Fig. 83-8. Battle-ax warriors
(Mural on the east wall of the antechamber, Anak Tomb No. 3 in Anak, North Korea)

Fig. 83-9. Battle-axes
(Guui-dong Fort in Seoul, Seoul National University Museum)

Fig. 84-1. Shields
(Corridor mural, eastern side of the burial chamber, Anak Tomb No. 3 in Anak, North Korea)

without ornaments, inscribed with three leaves, and inscribed with a dragon or phoenix. Battle-axes were originally used to chop trees, but in ancient societies were also used as weapons. Tomb murals depict people carrying spears, swords and battle-axes on their shoulders during military marches.

Armor

The armor suit, helmet and shield were made of iron to protect soldiers from enemy attacks (fig. 84). Goguryeo suits of armor were made either of iron or leather and consisted of many iron

Fig. 84-2. Helmet
(Fort No. 4 on Mt. Achasan in Seoul,
Seoul National University Museum)

Fig. 84-3. Armor suit pieces
(Fort No. 4 on Mt. Achasan in Seoul,
Seoul National University Museum)

scales. Helmets were manufactured with pieces left over from the suit of armor and the greater the ornamentation on the helmet indicated the higher the individual's status.

Unlike the infantry who wore lighter battle gear, the cavalry had to wear heavily armored jackets, pants and helmets. As their role kept them at the front of the battle lines, they faced an increased risk of capture or death. Usually the cavalry wore iron scale armor to protect their body while enabling them to move freely. Given the danger, their horses also were clad in armor suits and helmets (fig. 85). The battle capability of the armored cavalry was much higher than unarmored men and horses, but it was difficult for the state to maintain a large troop of armored cavalry due to the high cost. Thus, elite armored cavalry units were only dispatched to major battles. The presence of Goguryeo armored cavalry is very significant in that it shows the level of development of iron manufacturing and the iron industry of Goguryeo.

Battles

In ancient society, a battle started when two generals of the two states confronted one another in person. *Nihon shoki* (日本書紀), a historical chronicle from Japan, describes in detail a

Fig. 85-1. Armored cavalry
(Corridor mural, eastern side of the burial chamber, Anak Tomb No. 3 in Anak, North Korea)

Fig. 85-2. Armored cavalry
(Mural on the east wall of the antechamber, Deokheung-ri Mural Tomb in Nampo, North Korea)

Fig. 86-1. Battle (replica)
(Mural on the north wall of the first burial chamber, Samsilchong in Ji'an, China)

Fig. 86-2. Beheading
(Mural on the north wall of the burial chamber, north chamber of Tonggu Tomb No. 12 in Ji'an, China)

battle scene between Goguryeo and Baekje. When the two armies met in the field, they sent their generals forward. The two generals, on horseback and fully armored, discussed their ancestral lineage back to four generations, to determine whether or not they could contend on equal footing. When determined as acceptable, single combat between the two generals ensued (fig. 86). In most cases, this one-on-one fight determined which state was to be victorious. In the case of no surrender from either side, soldiers from each side were drawn into a full-scale battle. In the case of attack against a fortress, an all-out war was waged with soldiers and generals together.

II

Outline of the
Goguryeo History

Foundation

1

Indications of Goguryeo's founding started to emerge about 30 years after Guryeo people drove out the commanderies set up by the Chinese Han Dynasty. In 75 B.C., Han China, which had failed to confront the Guryeo natives, moved the Xuantu Commandery (玄兔郡), originally located in the middle of the Amnokgang river (鴨綠江) basin, to the Suzihe river (蘇子河) in the northwest, and then to the Liaodong area. As a result, the Guryeo confederation of small states was formed in Jolbon (卒本, now Huanren) and other regions. These small states entrusted the most powerful state with representational authority and also recognized the autonomy and territory of each state. When a group of Guryeo people led by Jumong, the legendary founder of Goguryeo, left Buyeo for the Biryusu (沸流水) region, Songyang (松壤) state was designated as the leader of the confederated small states in the Biryusu region.

The scope of the confederation in the Amnokgang river region expanded as people fled their homelands in Buyeo and Eastern Buyeo to migrate to Guryeo lands. The expelled commanderies of Han Dynasty attempted to reoccupy the territory as Northern Buyeo also struggled to seize Guryeo territory. In addition, the Nangnang Commandery(樂浪郡) in the south sought an opportunity to establish its own commandery in the region.

Around that time, a group headed by Jumong from Buyeo had reached Biryusu. King Songyang (松壤王), who ruled the Jolbon region, realized that the group's leader was of the Buyeo royal family and was in fact Jumong renowned for his prowess at the bow, as his nickname "skilled archer" indicated. The king allowed Jumong's group to settle a nearby Jolboncheon river; he also gave his daughter Soseono(召西奴) in marriage to Jumong. This illustrates a part of Buyeo migration history which occurred mid-first century B.C. in the Biryusu basin that flows into the middle section of which occurred the Amnokgang river.

Before long, the group's modest settlement in a corner of Jolbon led to the foundation of the new state of "Goguryeo."

The more powerful five states among the small political entities called *naguk*(那國) united to defend the Guryeo territory against neighboring forces. As Jumong had been the acknowledged leader, these five powers appointed him as the first king of the new state in Holbon(忽本, Jolbon).

As many small states, including the five powers, had united to form Goguryeo, harmony and unity was of utmost importance. Each was well aware that if any backstabbing or rivalry arose, their hard-won state could be easily divided, disintegrated and once again under Buyeo control. Therefore, to ensure their state's future, the Dongmaeng festival(東盟祭)— a state congress in which aristocrats and *daein*(大人, leaders) met to consult together on state affairs, make decisions, and pass judgment on severe crimes— was held annually alongside the Amnokgang river. Goods and items necessary for rituals and national administration were also collected at the Dongmaeng, demonstrating the pride the people felt in the new kingdom of Goguryeo and their leader Jumong.

In 3 B.C., King Yuri(琉璃明王), Jumong's successor, decided to leave Jolbon because the area was still vulnerable to attacks from Xianbei (鮮卑) tribes and Buyeo despite being ringed by high mountains. Furthermore, as the site was geographically limited in terms of its potential to develop into a large city, the capital was moved to Gungnaeseong. The move came as Eastern Buyeo forces attacked Goguryeo in 6 B.C. and after the death of the Crown Prince Dojeol(都切) who refused to be taken hostage by Eastern Buyeo. After relocating, Goguryeo continued to aggressively conquer other regions, benefiting from the excellent defense capabilities and superior transport infrastructure (in particular, the Anmokgang river) of the new capital. Buyeo, however, continued to harrass Goguryeo even after the capital's relocation.

King Daemusin(大武神王), King Yuri's successor, undertook the construction of the tomb of King Dongmyeong (東明聖王, Jumong) to gather public support for his reign. After deterring an attack from Buyeo, which was concerned about Goguryeo's rapid growth, the king led expeditionary forces to strike at Eastern Buyeo. He had interpreted the discovery of a crow with two bodies and one head as a sign that Goguryeo would successfully occupy Eastern Buyeo. Despite the invasion's failure, the king did succeed in permanently discouraging Eastern Buyeo from further military incursions by killing King Daeso(帶素王), the last king of Eastern Buyeo.

After Eastern Buyeo lost its grip on power, no Yemaek tribes remained that were powerful enough to obstruct Goguryeo's outward expansion in southern Manchuria and the northern part of the Korean peninsula. During the reign of King Daemusin, forces led by Prince Hodong (好童) conquered Nangnang in the south. Records in *Samguk sagi* describe the tragic love story between the Princess of Nangnang and Prince Hodong of Goguryeo.

"When Prince Hodong was in the Okjeo region, he met the king of the Nangnang, Choe Ri (崔理). The king said, 'You do not seem like an ordinary man. I wonder if you are a son of the Divine King of the northern state (Goguryeo).' He took the prince as his son-in-law. After the prince returned to his state, he sent a secret messenger to his wife with the following message: 'I will welcome you if you destroy the drum and the trumpet in the weapons chamber. If not, I will not accept you as my wife.' He knew that the drum and the trumpet in the Nangnang arsenal automatically signaled whenever an enemy approached. So the princess, following her husband's command, destroyed the musical instruments. The king then lost the battle because he did not hear the drum and the trumpet. Later, the king killed his daughter and surrendered."

As Goguryeo was developing into a state with its own system, rulers of *daenaguk* or *nabu* (大那國 or 那部 a political unit which united many *na* states), naguk(那國, a political unit which ruled over many *na* groups), and *na* groups were given official positions called *paeja*(沛者), *utae*(優台) and *joui*(皂衣). Leaders of small or large political entities were called *ga* (加), with *jega hoeui*(諸加 會議, a meeting of many *ga*) serving as the decision-making council. Of course, voting rights were granted according to rank. *Daega*(大加, great *ga*) donned unique hats called *chaek*(幘) and *soga* (小加, small *ga*) and those with less influence wore scone-shaped hats called *jeolpung*(折風) so that their status and official position were easily recognizable.

However, as royal authority remained weak, *daega*, governors of *nabu*, governed their own enclaves supported by their own officials such as called *saja* (使者), *joui* (皂衣), and *seonin* (先人). *Saja* controlled many other groups and collected goods and items following orders from the *daega*.

The sixth King Taejo (太祖王) pushed forcefully to conquer neighboring kingdoms and led Goguryeo to Eastern Okjeo and Northern Okjeo which lay beyond the Gaema Plateau. He also dispatched his army to the cities under the control of the

Xuantu Commandery and Liaodong Commandery in the west, continuing to expand both territory and royal authority. King Taejo became the first king to transform the confederation of five *nabu* into a true kingdom (map 1).

Now the *nabu* could no longer exercise their power as a state within the larger state. The *daega*, who once enjoyed privileges equivalent to those of a king, had no choice but to serve the king of Goguryeo, even though they still retained their own governing system. Since only the descendents of King Taejo were now considered eligible for the throne, the Ko family of the Gyeru lineage (桂樓部) monopolized the throne. During the reign of King Gogukcheon (故國川王), royal succession was patrilineal instead of fraternal.

At the end of the second century, a growing number of people —burdened by local tributary payments known as *gongnap* (貢納) and often displaced and poverty-stricken due to natural disasters—were recruited for labor related to missions of conquest. In the autumn of 194, on his way to go hunting, King Gogukcheon encountered a young man weeping on the street. When the king stopped to ask the young man why he was crying, the man replied: "I used to work as a day laborer to

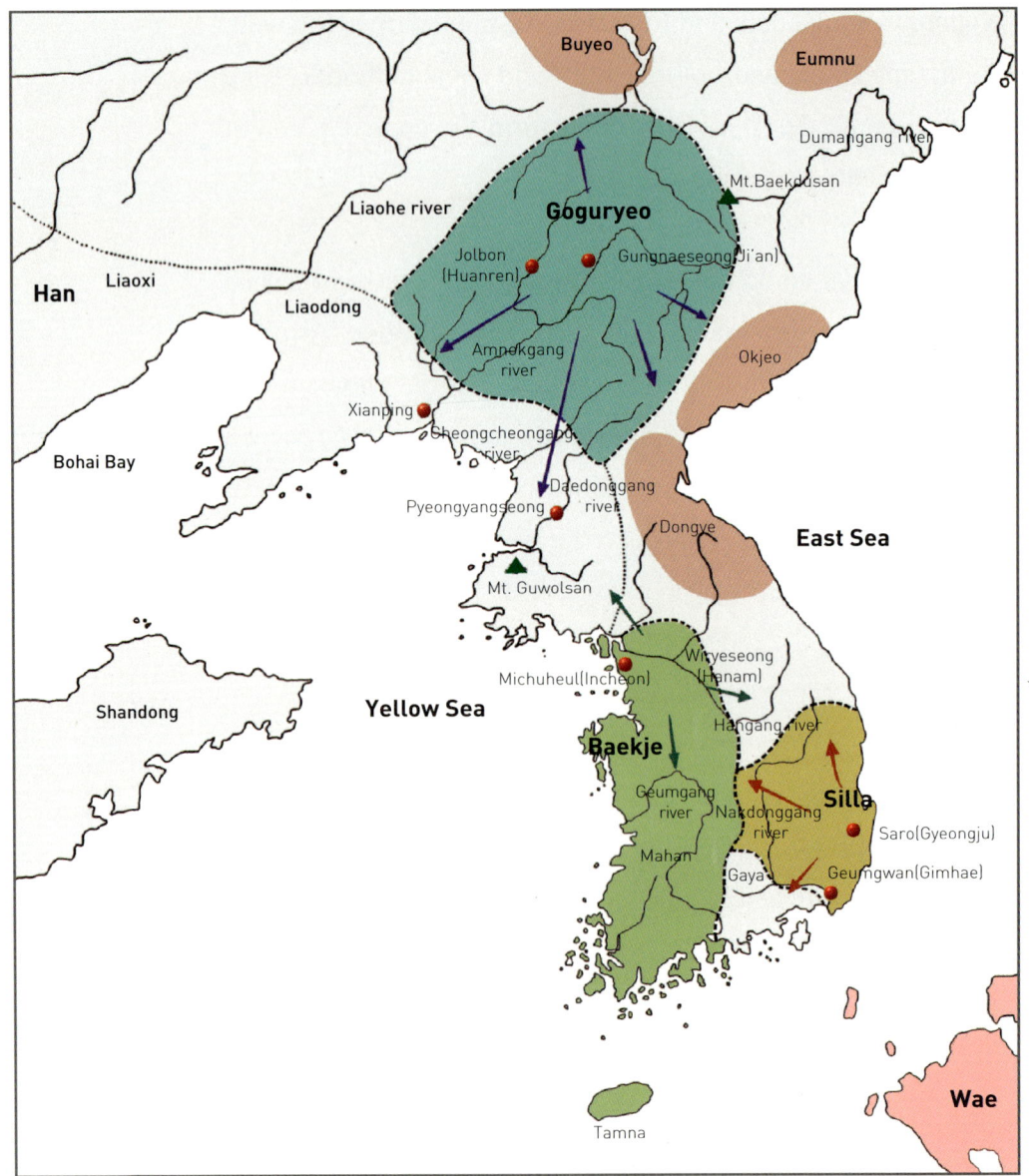

Map 1. Foundation and growth

support my mother but now I can't even get a handful of grain because of the poor harvest this year." The king himself took responsibility for the situation and gave the man clothes and food out of sympathy. Afterwards, he ordered his ministers to implement a system called Jindaebeop (賑貸法, Relief Loan Law), which enabled poor people to borrow grain from the government in the spring, to be repaid with some interest after the autumn harvest.

When King Sansang (山上王) ascended the throne, he married Lady U, the widow of his brother, the previous King Gogukcheon. Under a fraternal rather than a patrilineal royal succession system, Lady U was instrumental in Yeonu (King Sansang) becoming king instead of Balgi, the first younger brother of King Gogukcheon. In fact, the practice in which a younger brother takes his deceased brother's widow as his wife and supports his brother's bereaved family had been a longstanding tradition. However, when Lady U died, she left a will stating that she wanted to be buried next to King Sansang's grave, not her previous husband's. This indicates that this marital tradition disappeared by the early third century.

Fig. 87. Sanseongha Tombs in Ji'an, China

In the beginning of the third century, China was racked by
divisions and had entered into the Three Kingdoms period.
King Dongcheon (東川王) was looking for an opportunity to
advance into Liaodong and sought to benefit from the political
instability in China. Goguryeo, with 5,000 warriors each
equipped with iron weapons, yearned to conquer the Liaodong

peninsula which was temporarily outside of China's concern. In 242, the Goguryeo army attacked Xianping (西安平) on the peninsula, but to no avail, because Commander Guan Qiujian (毌丘儉) of Wei (魏) had anticipated the assault and counterattacked. The soldiers were forced to retreat, Gungnaeseong and Hwando Mountain Fortress (丸都山城) were overrun, and King Dongcheon and his court escaped to Northern Okjeo on the east coast.

After the death of King Dongcheon, who had showed his courage in personally leading the war against Wei, many subjects attempted to follow him in death (fig. 87). Although the new King Jungcheon (中川王) attempted to prohibit such suicides, the former king's followers buried themselves alive in the tomb of the deceased king on the day of the funeral according to Goguryeo custom at that time (map 2).

Map 2. Northeast Asia in the third century

Growth

2

In the late third century, Goguryeo kings started to centralize and strengthen royal authority, making strenuous efforts to control *nabu* based on royal power. As for leaders of *nabu* unable to mobilize their independent governance structures, it was more advantageous to become aristocrats, or persons close to the king. The officials under the control of the *nabu* were absorbed into the state organization which would rule the people of the *nabu*.

Leaders of *nabu* came to actively engage in the centralized kingdom in order to regain the power and wealth that they had previously enjoyed, and accordingly moved to the capital. The official ranks granted to the leaders of *nabu* were discarded and the new official rank system of *hyeong* group and *saja* group was implemented in its stead, subsequently integrated into the unified rank system.

The previous *nabu* system had been divided into a number of local administrative districts. The administrative district of *gok* (谷) was based on a unit of valleys along the river, with new districts set up along major roads and fortified by newly constructed fortresses. Local officials were dispatched to major districts and army forces stationed in those districts as well. Goguryeo in the early fourth century was transformed into a state equipped with a multi-dimensional defense system focused on the fortress and a military system that could mobilize hundreds of thousands of soldiers at a time.

In 317, with the collapse of Western Jin (西晉), the northern nomadic tribes in China began to migrate and expand their territories in earnest, and northern China fell into chaos; this was the beginning of the Sixteen Kingdoms period. King Micheon (美川王) hazarded a chance and made preparations to advance into Liaodong, a long-desired goal of his predecessors. King Micheon had once wandered on the banks of the Amnokgang river fearing that King Bongsang (烽上王), his eldest uncle, planned to kill him. As soon as King Micheon came to power, he occupied Xianping situated in the lower part of the river that links the Nangnang and Liaodong.

His experiences living near the river proved helpful in his conquest of the Liaodong region as he was very knowledgeable of the area's geography. King Micheon suceeded in his occupation of the Nangnang and Daifang(帶方郡) commanderies and part of Liaodong due to his strategy of blocking major roads. In the 330s, he also annexed Buyeo by the Songhuajiang river(松花江). It was during his reign that Goguryeo's territory extended from the "food basket" of the northwest of the Korean peninsula to the great plains near the Songhuajiang river in China. His experience before his rise to power has been memorably described in the *Samguk sagi*.

"When King Bongsang killed his brother Dolgo(突固) out of fear that his brother was turning against him, Dolgo's son, Eulbul(乙拂, King Micheon), fearing for his life, escaped and became a servant in Eummo's house in Susilchon(水室村). Eummo(陰牟), unaware of Eulbul's identity, treated him very harshly. For instance, he told Eulbul to throw pieces of roof tile and stones into a pond all night long to prevent the frogs from croaking. During the day, he had the impoverished prince chop firewood without a break. Eulbul had no choice but to run away from the house and sold salt with Jaemo(再牟) from Dongchon(東村). He unloaded salt when he arrived at the Amnokgang river and stayed at a house in Sasuchon (思收村) in the Gangdong (江東) region. When the old lady of the house in which he was staying asked him for a certain amount of salt, he gave it. But when she asked him over and over again, he refused. In revenge, the old lady hid her shoes in the bag of salt. When he got up to leave, the woman ran after him accusing him of stealing her shoes. She filed charges against him with the governor in the Amnokgang river area. The governor ordered Eulbul to give some salt to compensate for the stolen shoes and to be whipped on his buttocks and released. Nobody knew he was a member of the royal family because he looked so poor."

These experiences would prove invaluable in strengthening the state, drawing up national strategies for its development and implementing those policies.

After taking over the former territories of Gojoseon (古朝鮮) and Buyeo, King Micheon turned his eye westward to the Liaodong region which was then occupied by a state called Former Yan (前燕) that had been founded by the Murong tribe (慕容部) of Xianbei. Despite strategic alliances with Later Zhao (後趙) that occupied the Shandong, Hebei and Henan regions

Fig. 88. Jechong in Ji'an, China

and other Xianbei tribes — the Yuwon（宇文部）and Duan（段部）

tribes —, Goguryeo failed to overcome Liaodong in the end

(fig. 88).

After the death of King Micheon, the vision of Goguryeo expansion into Liaodong was passed down to the king's successor, King Gogugwon (故國原王). In the mid-fourth century, Goguryeo and Former Yan engaged in a series of small and larger scale skirmishes as they vied for control over the Liaodong and Buyeo regions. Former Yan did not want to be constricted by Goguryeo when it moved into the central China; and Goguryeo wanted to maintain the route toward Gungnaeseong and its bridgehead to the west.

In 342, Murong Huang (慕容皝) of Former Yan waged war against Goguryeo. King Gogugwon succeeded in keeping the Buyeo territories intact but failed to protect the capital. Anticipating that Goguryeo would defend even the northern road leading to Buyeoseong, the Former Yan forces instead directly advanced into Gungnaeseong via the difficult southern route. The result was that the royal palaces were burned, the tomb of King Micheon looted, and the king's mother and the queen along with 50,000 people were taken hostage by Former Yan.

After its defeat by Former Yan, Goguryeo decided to expand to the south while fixing its westbound border in place.

Foreign policy also shifted because the deceased king's body has not been returned to the state and his mother and wife continued to be held hostage by Former Yan. The 20,000 strong Goguryeo forces suffered immense losses in a rout by Baekje forces pushing northward. Led by Prince Geungusu (近仇首) and his father, King Geunchogo (近肖古王), the Baekje forces advanced north to defeat the Goguryeo forces and then came down to Pyeongyangseong. Goguryeo's King Gogugwon personally led his troops out to battle but was shot down with arrows and killed.

The king's death caused the state to review and revise its long maintained state system. In particular, the new king and aristocrats became increasingly aware that more than stopgap measures were needed if Goguryeo hoped to successfully manage a state with such a growing population.

The next ruler, King Sosurim (小獸林王), was determined that Goguryeo adapt to the demands of the era and the requirements for its level of power. Consequently, in 372 the new king officially accepted Buddhism, a combination of non-native culture, philosophy and religion, and established the Taehak (太學), an academy to foster capable bureaucrats.

During the early period of his reign, he promulgated a code of administrative laws called *yullyeong*(律令) which modified the Chinese ruling system. At last, a ruling ideology that focused on the king and other institutions had been installed as the framework for the preparation and implementation of effective governance structure.

King Gogugyang(故國壤王), the younger brother of King Sosurim, encouraged his people to have faith in the new state religion and maintain all royal shrines in good order. He also prevented aristocrats from claiming themselves to be descendents of Heaven. As such, only the royal family was considered descendents of Heaven and aristocrats accepted that by the sacred royal family had blessed them. Thus, the initial steps for Goguryeo's eventual domination of East Asia had been taken.

Expansion

3

During the era of King Gwanggaeto the Great (廣開土大王) of Goguryeo, northern China underwent a period of chaos now known as the "Sixteen Kingdoms of Five Ethnic Groups." Five nomadic groups, or the Xiongnu (匈奴), the Xianbei (鮮卑), the Jie (羯), the Di (抵), and the Qiang (羌), founded 16 states successively or simultaneously for approximately 120 years. Out of these, during the era of King Gwanggaeto the Great, there were seven states in existence. These nomadic dynasties formed diplomatic relations with one another in the fight for hegemony in northern China or sometimes just in a struggle for survival. It was not uncommon for wars and alliances to come and go as existing strong states were replaced with new ones. States situated across Hebei and Liaoning in China attempted to conquer Goguryeo as they advanced into central China. Thus, it was inevitable that conflicts arose between Goguryeo and those states with territorial ambitions toward the west.

At the age of 18, Prince Damdeok (談德, who later becomes King Gwanggaeto the Great), son of King Gogugyang, led an army to attack Baekje. The kingdom of Baekje, responsible for the death of the earlier King Gogugwon, was a major obstacle in Goguryeo's bid to become a superpower in East Asia. After his ascension to the throne, King Gwanggaeto successfully attacked Gwanmiseong Fortress (關彌城) located in the lower part of the Hangang river (漢江) basin and captured the capital of Hanseong (漢城), occupying Baekje lands, north of the Hangang river. In response, King Asin (阿莘王) of Baekje returned a number of hostages to Goguryeo and vowed to "serve Goguryeo forever."

When King Gwanggaeto the Great seized Qidan in the northwest and Sushen (肅愼) in the northeast of Manchuria and began preparations to move against Liaodong, he received a delegation from Silla asking for military support. In 399, the allied forces of Gaya (伽倻) and Japan backed by Baekje had invaded Silla and enveloped Geumseong (金城, Gyeongju today). One year later in 400, 50,000 Goguryeo soldiers traveled down to this southern region. After the Gaya-Japan allied army was defeated and Gaya's stronghold (Gimhae today) was devastated, the Gaya people migrated en masse to the islands of Japan.

Subsequently, the Goguryeo forces were stationed in Geumseong and Silla became a tributary state of Goguryeo.

King Gwanggaeto the Great subjugated the southern part of the peninsula and turned his focus to expansion into Later Yan (後燕, following Former Yan) which held the eastern and western regions of the Liaohe river (遼河) since 400. His plan was to advance into Liaodong. While Later Yan launched sporadic attacks against the Goguryeo host, in the end, King Gwanggaeto the Great was victorious over Later Yan and expanded his territory over the Liaohe river (fig. 89).

Fig. 89-1. Stele of King Gwanggaeto the Great in Ji'an, China (1920s)

Fig. 89-2. Stele of King Gwanggaeto the Great in Ji'an, China (2000s)

His 22-year reign led to recognization of Goguryeo as a strong power in northeast Asia. His terrain encompassed the Qidan territory on the eastern border of the Daxinganling Mountains in the northwest and the Liaohe river in the west. In the east, Goguryeo had jurisdiction over the forests in east Manchuria and in the south, over the Hangang and Nakdonggang rivers (洛東江) [map 3].

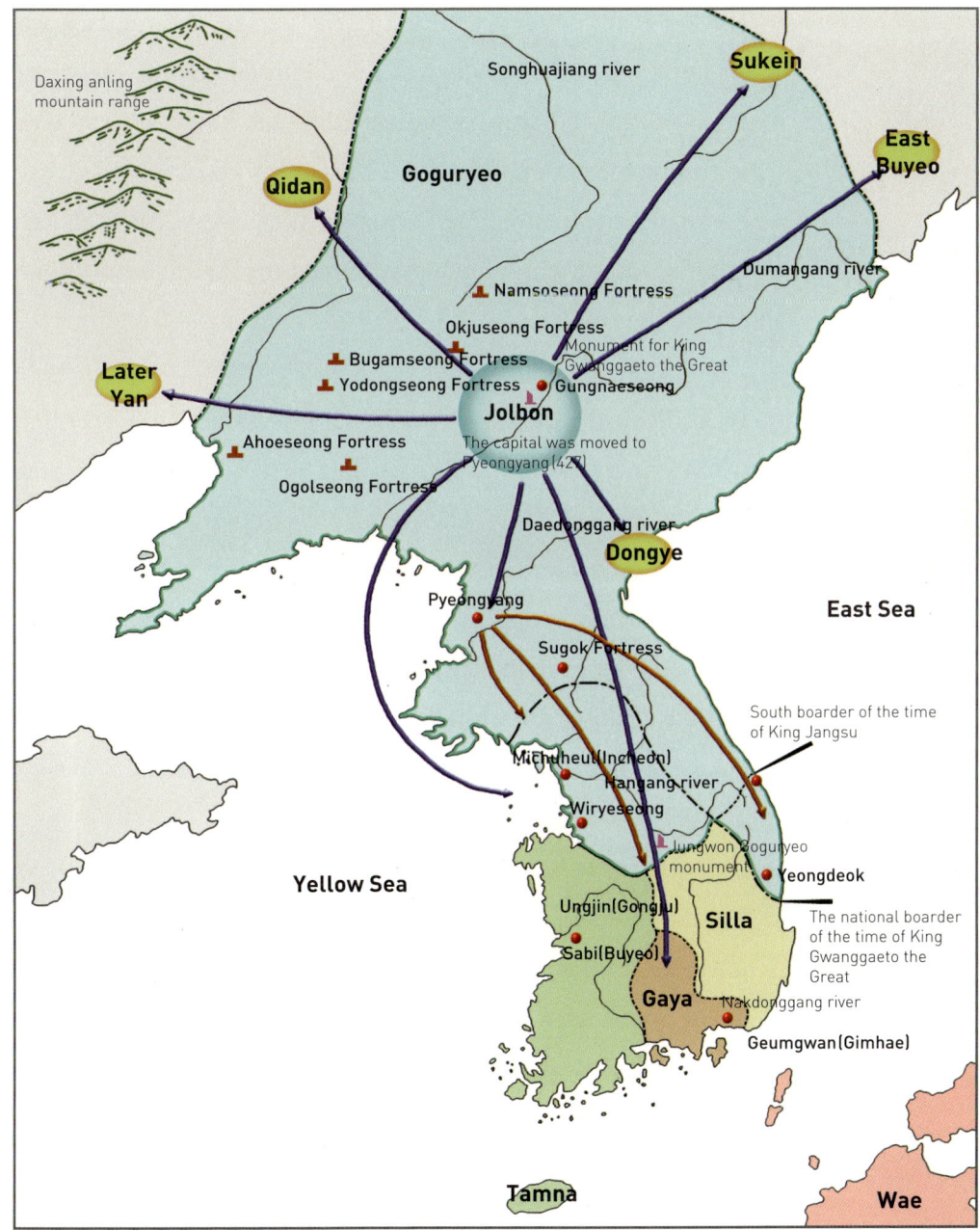

Daxing anling mountain range

Songhuajiang river

Sukein

East Buyeo

Qidan

Goguryeo

Dumangang river

Namsoseong Fortress

Okjuseong Fortress

Monument for King Gwanggaeto the Great

Later Yan

Bugamseong Fortress

Yodongseong Fortress

Gungnaeseong

Jolbon

Ahoeseong Fortress

The capital was moved to Pyeongyang (427)

Ogolseong Fortress

Daedonggang river

Dongye

Pyeongyang

East Sea

Sugok Fortress

South boarder of the time of King Jangsu

Michuheul (Incheon)

Hangang river

Wiryeseong

Jungwon Goguryeo monument

Yellow Sea

Yeongdeok

Ungjin (Gongju)

Silla

The national boarder of the time of King Gwanggaeto the Great

Sabi (Buyeo)

Gaya

Nakdonggang river

Geumgwan (Gimhae)

Tamna

Wae

Map 3. Expansion

During King Gwanggaeto the Great's reign, the military was no longer the army of *bu* (enclaves) controlled by the aristocrats but a centralized army commanded by the king. Soldiers were to follow the commands of the king or his generals and always be ready to strike. Furthermore, they were divided into infantry, cavalry and navy and trained for the highest military capabilities.

In addition to the army itself, Goguryeo crafted excellent offensive and defensive arms due to developments in steel forging and smelting. The cavalry was comprised of knights and troops equipped with horses, iron armor and helmets. When manufacturing the armor, Goguryeo artisans punctured miniscule holes in the small iron panels, connecting them with leather string so that they resembled fish scales. The scale-shaped armor was light and resistant against external impact.

In many regards, the iron-forged arms used by the Goguryeo forces were superior to those used by neighboring states. The arrowheads and axes excavated from a fort in Gui-dong (九宜洞) of Seoul near the Hangang river have been found to have been made of strong steel containing 0.86 percent carbon. Therefore, it is evident that Goguryeo soldiers set off for battle with excellent operational strategies and high-quality equipment.

In 413, when King Jangsu(長壽王) succeeded King Gwanggaeto the Great, the chaos in northern China had almost come to an end. States such as Northern Yan(北燕) and Northern Liang(北涼) lingered but Northern Wei(北魏) founded by the Tuoba clan (拓跋部) of the Xianbei tribe was on the verge of unifying the region. Following the defeat of Northern Yan located in Liaoxi, Goguryeo and Northern Wei found themselves looking over a common border.

Thus, Goguryeo faced preparations for possible conflict with Northern Wei. At that time, Goguryeo had already been recognized as an empire as a result of several conquests. Goguryeo's capital, Gungnaeseong, was no longer large enough to accommodate the growing population and quantities of traded goods. King Jangsu, therefore, decided to move the capital to Pyeongyang, which had already served as the secondary capital since the era of King Gwanggaeto the Great. So began the great project to move the capital to Pyeongyang from Gungnaeseong, which had been Goguryeo's political, social and cultural center for over 400 years.

In 436, Northern Wei and Goguryeo confronted each other at Longcheng(龍城), the capital of Northern Yan. According to the request from Feng Hong(馮泓), the last emperor of Northern Yan, the 20,000 strong Goguryeo forces arrived at Longcheng before the Northern Yan forces and led the Northern Yan emperor, aristocrats and common people safely out of the capital. The length of the refugee train stretched out over 80 *li* (about 31.5 km). Northern Wei forces were overwhelmed by the Goguryeo army and had no choice but to permit the mass exodus. Northern Wei, poised to unify northern China, had no desire to confront this strong empire, Goguryeo.

Due to this maneuver, Goguryeo and Northern Wei established peaceful diplomatic relations and acknowledged each side's power and territory. During the short period when Feng Hong of Northern Yan was attempting to restore his power, some conflict arose among Northern Wei of North China, Song(宋) of South and Goguryeo, but even that eventually ended with Goguryeo and Song's agreement to contain Northern Wei. Goguryeo, Rouran(幽然) and the Chinese Southern and Northern Dynasties became the four major powers in East Asia, an acknowledgment of Goguryeo's power in northeast Asia (map 4).

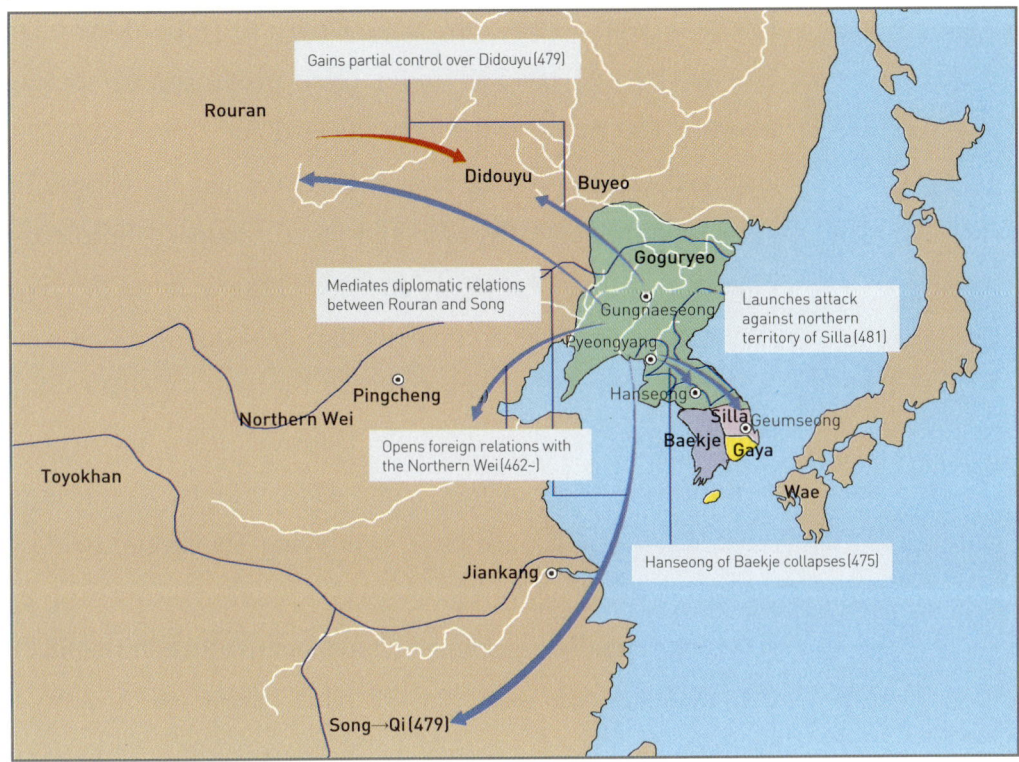

Map 4. East Asia in fifth century

After the stabilization of the western border, King Jangsu turned his attention to the south. In 475, he led his army against Baekje after the Silla-Baekje alliance had been formed to counteract threats posed by Goguryeo. The king first secured the western border by resuming diplomatic relations with

Northern Wei. Afterwards, King Jangsu dispatched the monk Dorim (道琳) to Baekje under false pretenses of seeking asylum. The monk gained trust from King Gaero (蓋鹵王) of Baekje due to his skill in Korean checkers and encouraged the king to remodel fortresses and royal palaces, build royal mausoleums, and construct an embankment along the river. While these large-scale construction projects signified royal authority, they also emptied out the state's coffers and impoverished the Baekje people. Dorim returned to Goguryeo to inform his king of the results. Accordingly, King Jangsu ordered an assault on Baekje, occupying Hanseong, Baekje's capital, killing King Gaero and advancing south of the Hangang river. Baekje had no choice but to move the capital to Ungjin (熊津, Gongju today). In 481, King Jangsu led his army to northern Geumseong, causing Silla to reconfirm Goguryeo's leadership in northeast Asia (fig. 90).

King Jangsu's drive for expansion continued for 64 years. He annexed the eastern region of the Didouyu (地豆于), a steppe tribe that resided at the border between eastern Mongolia and Manchuria. In addition, Goguryeo also incorporated a part of Gyeonggi-do province in the southern area of the Hangang river, which had been Baekje territory. After Goguryeo

Fig. 90. Reconstruction of Fort No. 4 on Mt. Achasan in Seoul
(Choi, Jong-taek).

vanquished and killed King Gaero in battle, Baekje was forced to move southward. Goguryeo's influence on the Mohe tribes in the northeast forests of Manchuria was strengthened and the scope of influence expanded. As a result, only the Heishui Mohe (黑水靺鞨) tribe, situated along the Amur River (黑龍江, Heilongjiang), remained outside the influence of Goguryeo.

4

Conflicts, Collapse and Succession

When King Munja (文咨明王) acceded to the throne after King Jangsu, Goguryeo's conquests came to a standstill. The final territorial expansion was due to the Buyeo royal family seeking asylum from the Wuji (勿吉) of the Mohe tribe. Aristocrats then contended with one another for central and local official posts, which led to armed clashes for royal succession.

As conflicts intensified among the aristocrats in Goguryeo, Silla and Baekje established an alliance and reoccupied an area near the Hangang river, declaring they were no longer under Goguryeo's control. 300 years of fractious disorder in China also finally came to an end. In 587, news started to spread that the Chinese Sui (隋) dynasty Destroyed Northern Qi (北齊) and was about to conquer the Chen (陳) of the Southern Dynasty (map 5).

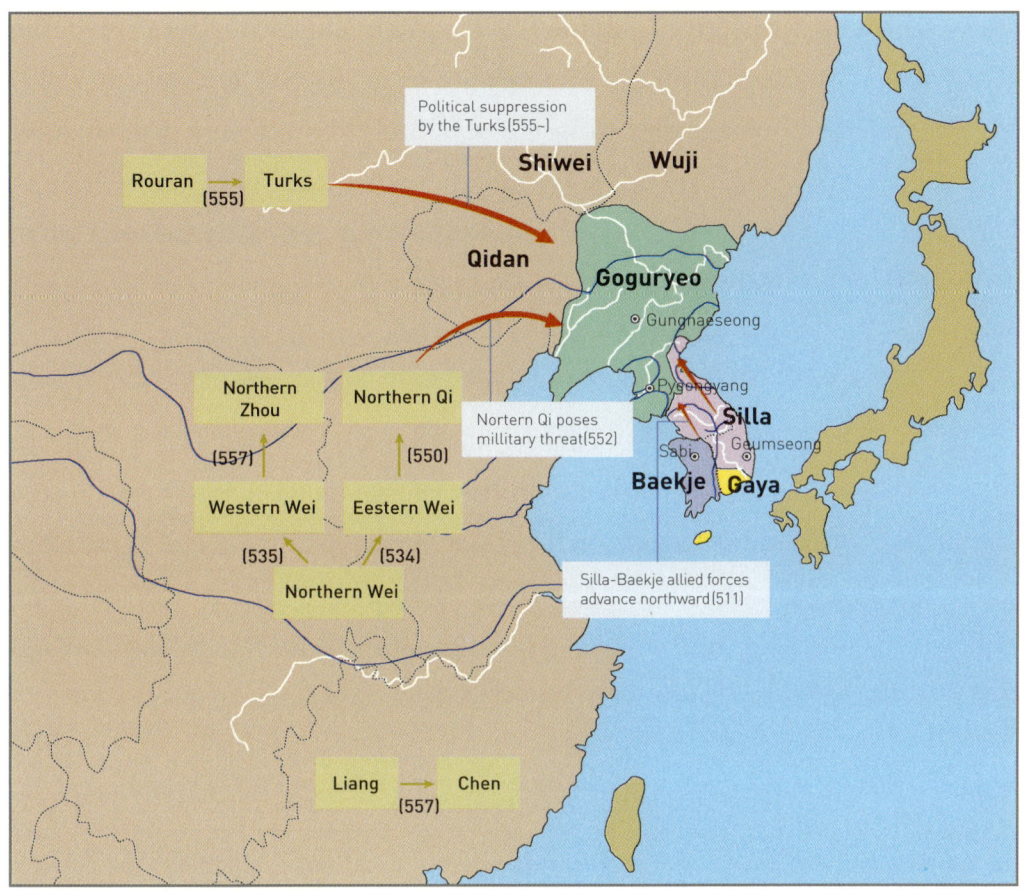

Map 5. East Asia in sixth century

The Goguryeo aristocrats came to a compromise for their coexistence with the reemergence of a unified China. They reinforced control over the Mohe and Qidan tribes, established a diplomatic strategy to seize the Sui Dynasty based on experiences from the period of "four powers of East Asia," and sent a group of envoys to the Turks and Chen. As expected, a unified China emerged with the end of the Southern and Northern Dynasties period when Jiankang(建康), the capital of Chen, was destroyed by the Sui army in 589.

Although Sui defeated the internally divided Turks, Goguryeo did not capitulate to the emboldened dynasty and instead waged a preemptive strike against Sui. In 598, the 10,000 strong Mohe army led by King Yeongyang(嬰陽王) invaded the Liaoxi region. Seemingly anticipating this, Sui in turn invaded Goguryeo with 300,000 soldiers, signalling the start of a war.

This first attack against Goguryeo was hampered in the Liaohe river. In 612, Sui mobilized three million combatants to assault Goguryeo. However, the Yodongseong Fortress proved impregnable. A detached force of 300,000 soldiers assaulted Pyeongyangseong but was defeated by the tactics of Eulji Mundeok (乙支文德), the Goguryeo general. When Sui attempted to cross the Liaohe river in 613 and 614, Goguryeo successfully protected its territory both times, resulting in many Sui casualties. Sui's failures triggered a series of large-scale rebellions and the eventual collapse of the dynasty.

In 618 with the defeat of Sui, Prince Geonmu (建武), who had halted the Sui advance to Pyeonyangseong, became the 26th Goguryeo king, King Yeongnyu (榮留王). In an attempt to knit together the disintegrated state, the king exchanged peace envoys with Chinese Tang (唐) and built an approximately 400-kilometer wall named Cheolli Jangseong (千里長城) along the border to prepare for possible attacks. In addition, the king strengthened royal authority by controlling the aristocrats.

Yeon Gaesomun (淵蓋蘇文)'s family was the first to be controlled, but the king's attempt at limiting aristocratic power ultimately failed. In 642, Yeon Gaesomun, who was appointed as the supervisor to oversee the building of the Cheolli Jangseong wall, staged a coup with other aristocrats, taking over the throne. The king, along with more than 180 aristocrats, were killed and thrown into a ditch.

In October of 644, the Tang forces started to cross the border of Goguryeo under the pretext of punishing Yeon's revolt. Over three months, the Tang army destroyed the major defense

Fig. 91-1. Gogeomji Mountain Fortress in Liaoning, China

Fig. 91-2. Deungnisa Mountain Fortress in Liaoning, China

points of Gaemoseong (蓋牟城), Yodongseong (遼東城), Bisaseong (卑沙城) and Baegamseong (白巖城) fortresses. They also defeated the 150,000 strong Goguryeo forces. If Tang could bring down the Ansiseong (安市城) fortresses, it would not have to worry about possible attacks from Goguryeo forces when crossing the Amnokgang river (fig. 91).

However, the Ansiseong fortress withstood a long siege for months without outside military support, contrary to Emperor Taizong (太宗)'s expectations. Rather than taking the battle outside the fortress, the commander and his soldiers remained inside and focused on protecting the fortress. In response, the Tang forces began to construct earth mounds southeast of the fortress and after 60 days of labor by the more than 500,000 Tang soldiers, the mound was higher than the fortress wall. However, the Goguryeo forces then assaulted and took over the earth mound. Following the assault, cold wind blew from the north of the Liaodong plain, signaling the advent of winter. Water started to freeze and food supplies grew meager. Finally, Taizong ordered his forces to withdraw (map 6).

In 648, Kim Chun-chu (金春秋), Silla's prime minister, went to Tang when Yeon Gaesomun of Goguryeo refused to help Silla.

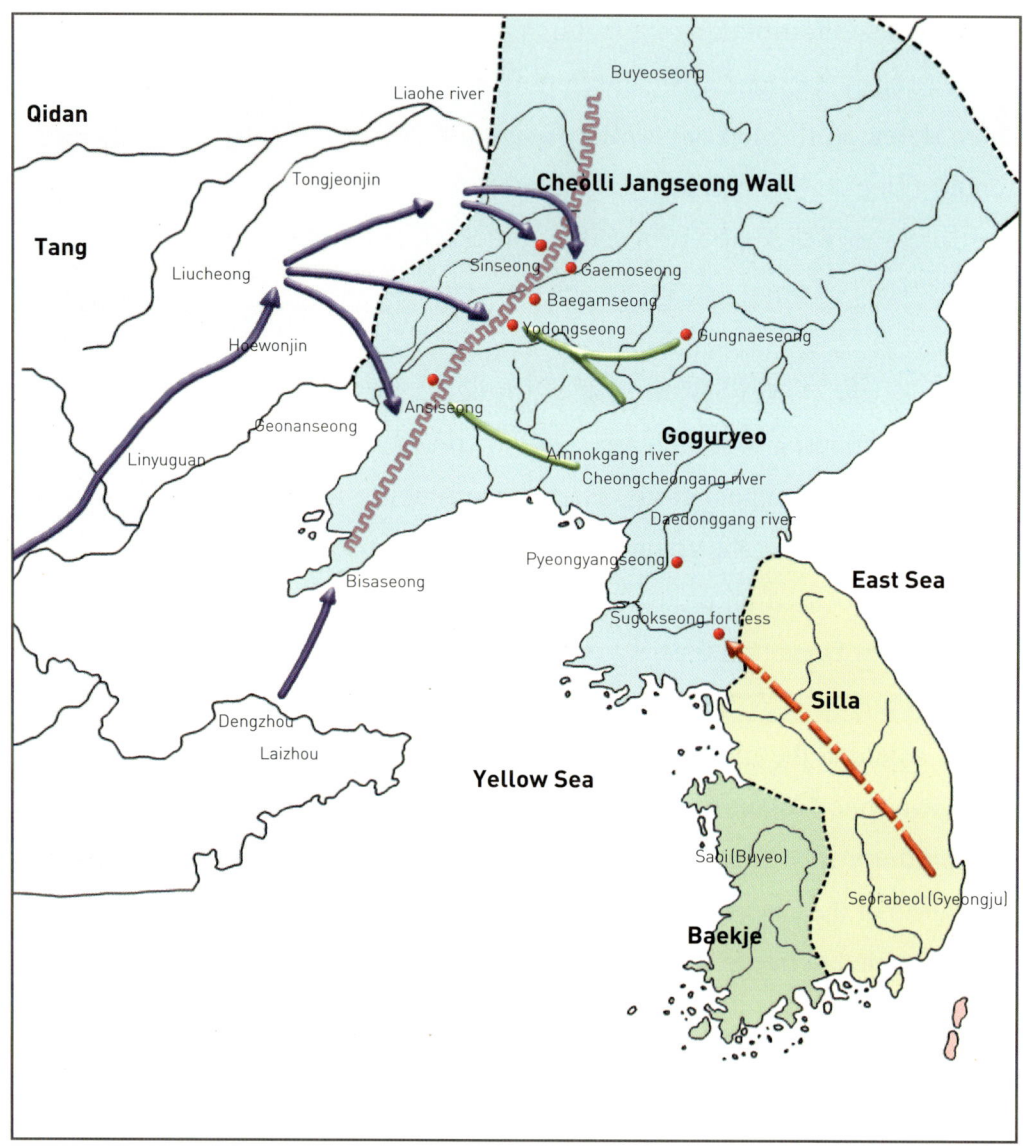

Map 6. War with Tang China (645)

Tang and Silla established a military alliance to eliminate Goguryeo and Baekje from the map. When Kim suggested "bringing down Baekje first and then striking Goguryeo," Taizong agreed.

After Baekje collapsed in 660, the Tang army launched an assault against Pyeongyangseong almost every year. Assisted by Silla, the Tang army did not have to worry about the food supply, the number one disadvantage for the Tang army. In 665, after the death of the dictator Yeon Gaesomun, aristocrats struggled to appoint a successor among the three sons of the deceased dictator. First, Yeon Namsaeng (淵男生), the eldest son, took power, but lost the throne to the hands of his two brothers and surrendered to Tang. And Yeon Jeongto (淵淨土), the younger brother of Yeon Gaesomun, also handed over his fortresses and his people to Silla and asked for asylum.

In 668, the Silla quartermaster corps headed to Pyeongyangseong with their food supply in thousands of ox-carts. Using the surrendered Yeon Namsaeng as a guide, Tang penetrated the defense line in Liaodong to attack Goguryeo fortresses. A few defense points including the Ansiseong fortress remained but the army in the enveloped Pyeongyangseong was exhausted.

In September of 668, King Bojang (寶藏王), the last king of Goguryeo, ordered Yeon Namgeon (淵男建), the youngest son of Yeon Gaesomun, and a group of aristocrats, to open the gate of Pyeongyangseong and send a message of surrender to the Tang commander. Over 700 years of Goguryeo had ended.

After the fall of Pyeongyangseong, Goguryeo aristocrats and professional artisans were taken to Tang and scattered across China. Others moved to the Mongol grasslands or even across the sea to Japan. Many refugees, who stayed in the former territory of Goguryeo, attempted to restore the state with the assistance of Silla. In 676, with the diplomatic reconciliations between Tang and Silla, some of the refugees escaped to Unified Silla and integrated within the new Silla, while others explored opportunities in Manchuria.

Another group resumed their determination to restore Goguryeo when the Qidan rebelled in Yingzhou (榮州) in the Liaoxi region in 692. That action led Dae Jo-yeong (大祚榮) to declare the foundation of Balhae (渤海) in 698. Within 30 years of Goguryeo's collapse, Balhae succeeded to Goguryeo's 700-year history and took the first step in reclaiming the kingdom's former territory.

III

Appendix

Captions

Chronological Timeline

References

Index

Captions

Fig. 1. Map of Janganseong Fortress

(Pyeongyang, North Korea)

Fig. 2-1. Gatekeepers (replica)

(Mural on the eastern and western sides of the north wall of the antechamber's entrance, Ssangyeongchong in Nampo, North Korea)

Two gatekeepers, wearing yellow *jeogori* (jacket) and red *baji* (pants) with black polka dots, stand toward the entrance, facing each other. The gatekeepers wear hats called *chaek* (幘) that are tied under their jaws, *jeogori* fastened in the front around the waist by ribbon, and large shoes with thick, upturned tips. Their posture is polite as they hold their hands together under their chests. Similar to figures on the passage wall, which are characterized with soft and refined brush lines, and other figures in the Susan-ri Mural Tomb, the gatekeepers have delicately delineated faces and steeply sloping, narrow shoulders.

Fig. 2-2. Gatekeepers

(Mural on the northern and southern sides of the east wall of the antechamber's entrance, Jangcheon Tomb No. 1 in Ji'an, China)

Two life-size gatekeepers stand on either side of the entrance, the one to the north is 153 cm tall and the one to the south is 155 cm tall. Unlike the figure on the north who gives off a scholarly impression because of his round face, gentle eyes, and courteous posture with his hands held together in front of his breast, the figure on the south appears much more warrior-like because of his square face, penetrating eyes, and a possibly threatening pose with his hands held in front of his abdomen.

Fig. 3-1. *Giwa* (Korean roof-end tile)

(Pyeongyang, Seoul National University Museum)

Fig. 3-2. Korean brick

(Pyeongyang, Seoul National University Museum)

Fig. 4. Reconstruction of *ondol* site

(Fort No. 4 on Mt. Achasan in Seoul, Choi, Jong-taek)

Fig. 5. Aristocratic residence

(Mural on the west wall of the burial chamber, Anak Tomb No. 1 in Anak, North Korea)

Fig. 6-1. Thirteen magistrates paying respects to the tomb occupant

(Mural on the west wall of the antechamber, Deokheung-ri Mural Tomb in Nampo, North Korea)

This is a portion of the mural where the *hyeollyeong* (縣令, magistrate) of Gye-hyeon (薊縣) and the *taesu* (太守, magistrate) of 13 *gun* (郡, counties) pay respects to the *jasa* (刺史, governor) of Yuju (幽州). Chinese characters next to the magistrates reveal their official posts and ranks. Written in front of the Yeon-gun magistrate (淵郡太守) are the following Chinese characters: "此十三郡屬幽州部縣七十五 州治廣薊今治燕國 去洛陽二千三百里 都尉一部并十三郡." These lines state that Yuju consists of 13 *gun* and 75 *hyeon*, that Yuju's administrative center is Gwanggye (廣薊), present-day Yeonguk (燕國), and that Yuju lies 2,300 *li* from Luoyang (洛陽).

No records or epigraph materials confirm whether Yuju consisted of 13 *gun* and 75 *hyeon* or in fact existed during the Chinese Wei, Jin and Sixteen Kingdoms periods. During the period of Northern and Southern Dynasties, dynasties would create semi-fictitious and semi-real administrative systems which included lands named for territory controlled by other kingdoms, in the form of *gyochi* (橋置). *Gyochi* refers to the adoption of the former name of the lands where new migrants resided before exile or war. As described in the above inscription, Yuju could be the combination of both real territory and imaginary territory. Scholars in North Korea understand the inscription as evidence that Goguryeo established an extensive territory called Yuju in northeastern China during the reign of King Gwanggaeto the Great.

The facial expressions of all thirteen magistrates are identical, making it impossible to distinguish each person's individuality. This may be in part due to limitations in the painter's skill, but also can be attributed to the era's artistic style that did not emphasize individuality.

Fig. 6-2. Governor of Yuju

(Mural on the north wall of the antechamber, Deokheung-ri Mural Tomb in Nampo, North Korea)

This is a portion of a mural where Governor Jin (鎭) of Yuju, the tomb occupant, is being saluted by magistrates from 13 *gun* while seated on a *pyeongsang* (low bench) in a *jangbang* (large curtained room). The tomb occupant wears *dopo* (Korean formal attire) as well as *nagwan* (the silk hat worn by aristocratic officials), sitting upright in his seat with a feather fan in his hand. The *nagwan*, an outer hat placed over an inner hat, is only worn by kings or high-ranking officials whose status can be distinguished by the color of *na* (羅, silk). The *nagwan* worn by the tomb occupant is perhaps the *cheongnagwan* (青羅冠, blue silk hat) worn by a minister. In order to depict the difference in status, male and female servants who play instruments behind the tomb occupant, wave large fans, or take orders from him are represented as smaller than the occupant.

Fig. 6-3. Tomb occupant

(Mural on the north wall of the burial chamber, Deokheung-ri Mural Tomb in Nampo, North Korea)

Jin, the tomb occupant, is portrayed sitting upright on a wooden *pyeongsang* laid to one side of the curtained room. Civil and military officials wearing black *chaek* or black hemp headwear stand beside Jin, who wears *cheongnagwan* as an outer hat and holds a feather fan. Nothing else is depicted in the room, which is spacious enough to hold additional *pyeongsang*. Considering that a horse, groom, and officials are drawn outside of the curtained room on the west of the north wall and that a covered ox-drawn carriage and servants are painted on the east, it is likely the empty space next to Jin is reserved for his wife. If she had been alive during the tomb construction, she would not have been pictured as residing in the spirit world.

Fig. 7-1. Battle-ax warriors

(Mural on the lower part of the eastern side of the antechamber's south wall, Anak Tomb No. 3 in Anak, North Korea)

Four warriors carrying battle-axes in their hands stand in a row, all wearing white *chaek* on their heads, long *jeogori* (jackets), and *baji* (pants) tied at the waist. Red *seon* (trim) are attached to their collars, jackets, and sleeves. Some figures wear *jeogori* with long breast-ties. Their faces resemble those of the standard-bearers in other murals and lack individuality. During ancient times, battle-axes were important weapons and also regarded as a symbol of the right of command.

Fig. 7-2. Standard-bearers

(Mural on the upper part of the eastern side of the antechamber's south wall, Anak Tomb No. 3 in Anak, North Korea)

Seven standard-bearers are lined up facing right. Four at the front of the procession wear long topcoats called *durumagi*, belted at their waists, and grasp standards. The three at the rear wear jackets and baggy pants of different colors and hold up a tasseled rod indicating the occupant's status, a streamer standard, and a parasol. To the right of the first standard-bearer, two Chinese characters are written in red: "戰吏" (lower official for war). The seven standard-bearers all have quite similar faces in shape and appearance and all wear *chaek* on their heads.

Fig. 7-3. Tomb occupant

(Mural on the west wall of the western side chamber attached to the antechamber, Anak Tomb No. 3 in Anak, North Korea)

Seated on a *jwasang* (a chair with long legs) in a curtained room, the tomb occupant either gives orders or receives briefings from his civil and military officials. His long wide face and neatly stretched handlebar moustache effectively portray a dignified appearance. He has a high-bridged nose, narrow eyes, and thick eyebrows. The tomb occupant's face was repainted three times or more and his eyes repositioned, most likely to widen the middle of the forehead for a magnanimous and benign expression. It is apparent to the naked eye that his hands and sleeve trim were also changed several times. The tomb occupant wears a white *deotgwan* (outer hat) over a black *naegwan* (inner hat) and in his right hand holds a feather fan called *jumi* with a carved goblin-face handle.

On the right side of the curtained room is an official royal standard called *jeol*. To the left and right of the tomb occupant are a figure who appears to be writing something with a brush, a figure who appears to be briefing the occupant, and others. Each figure—whether tomb occupant, civil or military officer, or servant—is sized differently according to his or her rank. Next to the figure holding a brush, the Chinese characters "記室" are written in red, by the figure holding a wooden mace "小史," behind the head of a figure who kneels with a document in his hands "省事," and by the figure beside him "門下排."

Fig. 7-4. Tomb occupant's wife and her servants

(Mural on the north wall of the western side chamber attached to the antechamber, Anak Tomb No. 3 in Anak, North Korea)

Within a curtained room, a noblewoman is seated on a *pyeongsang* (low bench) facing the tomb occupant. Servants attend the woman, two on her right and one in front. One of the servants on the left holds a rectangular fan, while the other holds her hands in front of her abdomen. The servant facing the noblewoman holds a tray with an incense burner. The noblewoman and her servants all wear their hair in chignons, though the servant holding the incense burner has more elaborately decorated hair. As in other murals, respective size of each figure conveys the difference in social status.

The noblewoman has narrow eyes, small lips, and a very plump face, which is not typical of Goguryeo women. Her hair is tied up in a chignon that makes a semi-circle around her head, while her remaining hair is loose. Several accessories were used to decorate the hair. The patterns on her robe are also very ornate. Her face, dress and ornamentation exhibit typical characteristics preferred in paintings of Chinese noblewomen from Han to Wei dynasties.

Fig. 7-5. Tomb occupant and his wives (replica)

(Mural on the northeast wall of the burial chamber, (original) Gakjeochong in Ji'an, China; (replica) Sookmyung Women's University)

This mural originally depicted the tomb occupant and his two wives sitting in a large curtained room but has deteriorated to the point that the husband can no longer be discerned. In the photo and reproduction prepared during research in the 1930s, the husband faces forward, sitting on a *pyeongsang*, and the two wives obliquely face their husband, while kneeling on floor cushions. In the photo and reproduction, a table on which a bow and some arrows had been laid could be seen but now this portion of the wall painting has eroded. The wife sitting further from the tomb occupant is drawn slightly larger than the closest wife. Both wives have their own dinner tables and wear white headwear called *geongwik* (巾幗). Their hands are courteously held together in the front of their abdomens. In the wall painting, the male and female servants are drawn radically smaller to indicate their low status and positions.

Fig. 7-6. Tomb occupant and his wife

(Mural on the north wall of the burial chamber, Ssangyeongchong in Nampo, North Korea)

The tomb occupant and his wife, male and female servants, and a pair of Hyeonmu (Black Tortoise-Serpent) are painted on the north wall of the burial chamber. Gazing ahead, the tomb occupant sits upright with his hands held together in front of his chest. He wears an outer silk hat called *nagwan* over an inner hat. His face is pink and his lips are very reddish as if cosmetics have been applied. The details of his wife's face are unrecognizable due to deterioration of the mural; however, it can still be seen that her cheeks were adorned with *gonji*, the decorative spots of rouge.

This mural differs from arrangements of couples in other mural tombs of the fifth century such as Gakjeochong, Yaksu-ri Mural Tomb, Suryeopchong, etc., in that the tomb occupant is seated on the left and his wife on the right. Male and female servants are painted quite small, again, probably as a way to present their relative hierarchical status. Outside of the curtained room in which the tomb occupant and his wife sit, a pair of Hyeonmu are painted with distinctive tortoise shells. Serpents with wide scales coil around the tortoise's body from top to bottom. This figure is similar to the Hyeonmu in Daean-ri Tomb No. 1, in that the head and legs of the tortoise are not reptilian, but rather a ferocious mammal. Relatively little importance is placed on this pair of Hyeonmu which are the tutelary deity of the tomb occupant and his wife.

Fig. 8-1. Grand procession

(Corridor mural, northern and eastern sides of the burial chamber, Anak Tomb No. 3 in Anak, North Korea)

The procession starts from the corridor's east wall (10.13 meters in length and

2.01 meters in height), and continues toward the north wall. The rear of the procession at the south end is relatively well preserved; at its northern end, however, the figures and ceremonial implements and weapons are barely discernible. In the grand procession, only the front group and the middle group escorting the tomb occupant, who rides on an ox-drawn carriage, are portrayed. From the procession's formation, it can be easily estimated that the procession totals about 500 persons including the omitted rear group. The mural is an excellent depiction of the procession through a bird's-eye-view of several rows. Various functionaries and servants surround the tomb occupant's carriage in a concentric oval. Standard-bearers, servants, an instrumental music band, and mounted guards are placed in front of and behind the carriage. Archers, battle-ax men, swordsmen, and other soldiers flank either side of the carriage. The whole group is then escorted by a troop of infantry and cavalry.

Fig. 8-2. Outing of the tomb occupant and his wife

(Mural on the west wall of the burial chamber, Susan-ri Mural Tomb in Nampo, North Korea)
An aristocratic couple is watching acrobatics while on an excursion. The acrobats and the male and female servants who hold a large parasol for the couple are painted to be much smaller than the nobles; status and position can be ascertained accordingly. The occupant wears a *gwan* on his head and a long garment with wide sleeves, the hem of which touches the ground. In front of his face lies a rectangular space for explaining the occupant's title or the scene, but nothing is written in it. His wife's face is decorated with lip color and rouge on her cheeks; and she wears a *jeogori* (jackets) adorned with beautiful patterns, and *saekdong jureum chima* (a pleated skirt with

multicolored stripes). Her appearance and posture embody the typical Goguryeo noblewoman's elegance; and she holds her hands in front of her chest, which is one of the customs of the Goguryeo people. A page is holding a large, tall parasol over the wife's head. Servants wear long waist-length jackets and pleated skirts. The harmony between the *git* (collar), *doryeon* (cuff), the black *seon* (trim) around the sleeves, and the steep shoulder line exemplifies the pleasing aesthetics of jackets worn by Goguryeo women.

Fig. 9. Offering ceremony of the seven treasures to Buddha

(Mural on the east wall of the burial chamber, Deokheung-ri Mural Tomb in Nampo, North Korea)

A pond is painted on the north end of the east wall and an offering ceremony on the south end. Two large lotuses with thick red edges, are in bloom in the middle of the pond; out of 10 lotus petals, the interior of the rear five petals and the exterior of the front five petals are portrayed.

To the right of a large tree where the offering ceremony is being held, a figure wearing a black two-horned *chaek* kneels on a *pyeongsang* and stretches his hands toward the front. This may be Jin, the tomb occupant, who is supervising the event. Behind him stand two officials wearing black hemp headwear. The characters "此人爲中裏都督典知七寶 自然音樂自然飮食 有口之 燔口口口口" are written behind the officials, indicating that the tomb occupant performed this offering while he held the post of *jungnidodok*. To left of the tree, an official and a female servant stand side by side behind a page. On the lower part of the mural, two women stand opposite to four men facing north.

Fig. 10. Aristocratic residence

(Reconstruction from murals of Deokheung-ri Mural Tomb in Nampo, North

Korea)

Fig. 11-1. Kitchen and meat storehouse

(Mural on the east wall of the eastern side chamber attached to the antechamber, Anak Tomb No. 3 in Anak, North Korea)

In the eastern side chamber of Anak Tomb No. 3, a kitchen and a storehouse for meat are drawn in the middle of the east wall. The tile-roofed house on the left is the kitchen, where three women are absorbed in food preparation. A woman standing in front of a large jar shaped like a *siru* (earthenware steamer) stirs the inside of the jar with a bar-like tool in her left hand, while holding a short-handled dipper with her right hand. Beneath the woman's right hand lies a small jar-like vessel, and above her head two Chinese characters are written: "阿婢." In front of the stoke hole of the *buttumak* (cooking fireplace), another woman builds the fire; and in the next compartment, a woman sets the meal table beside a small table piled with bowls. The *buttumak* in this mural has the same shape as clay and metal *buttumak* that have been unearthed from Goguryeo houses and tombs. In the garden, dogs are walking back and forth, while two birds perch on the roof of the kitchen. To the west of the kitchen, a roe deer, a pig, and other animals dangle from four large hooks inside the meat storehouse. Barely discernible Chinese characters "京屋" (storage) can be seen on the inside of the storehouse's left pillar.

Fig. 11-2. Carriage shed

(Mural on the east wall of the eastern side chamber attached to the antechamber, Anak Tomb No. 3 in Anak, North Korea)

Two carriages sit inside the two-room hip-roof structure. The left carriage has no awning, and has the same shape as the tomb occupant's carriage in the grand procession of the corridor mural. Below the inscription "犢車," the right-hand carriage is sheltered by an awning, and resembles a noblewoman's carriage depicted in the Deokheung-ri mural. In front of the carriage shed stands another red cart with an awning.

Fig. 11-3. Well

(Mural on the north wall of the eastern side chamber attached to the antechamber, Anak Tomb No. 3 in Anak, North Korea)

This mural is evidence that wells equipped with buckets, commonly found in some rural areas of Pyeongan-do province until just one generation ago, have existed for many centuries. Water jars of various shapes are placed beside the well and a manger can also be seen. One woman draws water from the well with a bucket while another fills jars with water. Above the woman's head is the inscription, "阿光." In addition, the Chinese character "井" is written above the well on the left.

Fig. 11-4. Mill

(Mural on the west wall of the eastern side chamber attached to the antechamber, Anak Tomb No. 3 in Anak, North Korea)

A treadmill lies inside a building. Two women wear their hair up; the woman on the left treads a long rod, while the woman on the right winnows the grains by hand. The Chinese character "碓" is written above the mill. The shape of the treadmill is almost identical to those still found in some rural areas in Korea.

Fig. 11-5. Cowshed

(Mural on the south wall of the eastern side chamber attached to the antechamber, Anak Tomb No. 3 in Anak, North Korea)

The hide colors of the three oxen eating from a manger differ from one another. The spotted one and the yellow one are busy eating, while the black one chews fodder with a relaxed, composed expression and looks back at its friends. Ox horns bent like bows and rising above their heads suggest water buffaloes, but their gentle eyes look like those of ordinary bulls found in the countryside today. An aristocratic family breeds the oxen in this cowshed for pulling carriages, not plows.

Fig. 11-6. Stable

(Mural on the west wall of the eastern side chamber attached to the antechamber, Anak Tomb No. 3 in Anak, North Korea)

Yellow, red, and white horses are portrayed eating hay from a stable manger. Saddles have been removed, and red bridles are slack beside their mouths. Their long thick manes cover their necks and the front of their shoulders, and their legs are short and strong. Each horse possesses a distinct expression: The yellow horse's eyes focus on the hay in the trough and the red horse gazes at the yellow one although its mouth is turned toward the manger. In front of the stable is a grazing area partitioned by a wooden fence.

Fig. 11-7. Stable and cowshed

(Mural on the south wall of the burial chamber, Deokheung-ri Mural Tomb in Nampo, North Korea)

On the western side of the south wall, a pond covers the left while a stable and a cowshed fill the upper and lower parts, respectively. Three horses stand side-by-side eating hay in the stable. As the manger is chest-high on the horses, they can eat without lowering their heads. The fairly large eyes of the horses have no particular expression. Their manes are not very thick, covering only their necks, their shoulders and rumps are rather bulky, and their legs are short and thin. If they are of the breed of horses popular in Goguryeo called *gwahama*(果下馬), said to have been so small that they could pass underneath fruit trees, their legs should be short and thick, and their manes should cover their shoulders. However, the three horses have no such characteristics. In the space to the left of the horses, the characters "此是 □ 前 厩養馬子" are written in Chinese ink. One man who appears to be the groom stands behind the horses, and the other two men gather and trim hay inside the stable. From their narrow pants and short-sleeved shirts, the men are probably household servants.

In the cowshed, two thick-bodied, thin-legged oxen eat forage from a manger. A wooden board in front of the manger hides the oxen's mouths, as perhaps the manger is too deep or they are hurriedly gobbling fodder. Behind the two oxen lie two carriages. One interpretation of this scene is the two oxen have just returned to the residence after pulling the noblewoman's carriage and have now been released to eat fodder.

Fig. 12. *Pyeongsang*

(Mural on the ceiling corbels of the burial chamber, Muyongchong in Ji'an, China)

Fig. 13. *Jwasang*

(Mural on the northeast wall of the burial chamber, Muyongchong in Ji'an, China)

Fig. 14. *Ondol*

(Fort No. 4 on Mt. Achasan in Seoul, Korea)

Fig. 15-1. Man

(Mural on the south wall of the first burial chamber, Samsilchong in Ji'an, China)

Fig. 15-2. Man

(Mural on the west wall of the antechamber, Deokhung-ri Mural Tomb in Nampo, North Korea)

Fig. 15-3. Man

(Mural on the north wall of the burial chamber, Susan-ri Mural Tomb in Nampo, North Korea)

Fig. 16-1. Woman

(Mural on the west wall of the burial chamber, Susan-ri Mural Tomb in Nampo, North Korea)

Fig. 16-2. Woman

(Mural on the south wall of the first burial chamber, Samsilchong in Ji'an, China)

Fig. 16-3. Woman

(Mural on the north wall of the burial chamber, Deokheung-ri Mural Tomb in Nampo, North Korea)

Fig. 17. Weaving woman (replica)

(Mural on the south wall of the burial chamber, Daean-ri Tomb No.1 in Nampo, North Korea)

This painting on the upper right side of the burial chamber's south wall shows a smiling woman gazing in the direction of the burial chamber as she sits in front of a loom to weave hemp cloth. This hemp cloth weaver may be considered as evidence supporting the possibility that the textile industry prospered during Goguryeo's prime around the mid-fifth century and the popularity of the myth of Jingnyeo (織女, Weaving Woman) among the people.

Fig. 18-1. *Gwan*

(Mural on the north wall of the burial chamber, Deokheung-ri Mural Tomb in Nampo, North Korea)

Fig. 18-2. *Chaek*

(Mural on the west wall of the antechamber, Deokheung-ri Mural Tomb in Nampo, North Korea)

Fig. 18-3. *Chaek*

(Corridor mural, eastern side of the burial chamber, Anak Tomb No. 3 in Anak, North Korea)

Fig. 18-4. *Jeolpung*

(Mural on the southeast wall of the burial chamber, Muyongchong in Ji'an, China)

Fig. 18-5. *Jeolpung*

(Mural on the south wall of the first burial chamber, Samsilchong in Ji'an, China)

Fig. 18-6. Hemp headwear

(Mural on the west wall of the burial chamber, Deokheung-ri Mural Tomb in Nampo, North Korea)

Fig. 18-7. Warrior's helmet

(Mural on the western side of the burial chamber's south wall, Anak Tomb No. 2 in Anak, North Korea)

Fig. 18-8. Topknot

(Mural on the east wall of the burial chamber, Yaksu-ri Mural Tomb in Nampo, North Korea)

Fig. 19-1. *Geongwik*

(Mural on the northeast wall of the burial chamber, Gakjeochong in Ji'an, China)

Fig. 19-2. *Geongwik*

(Mural on the south wall of the first burial chamber, Samsilchong in Ji'an, China)

Fig. 19-3. *Goriteun meori* **hairstyle**

(Mural on the north wall of the western side chamber attached to the antechamber, Anak Tomb No. 3 in Anak, North Korea)

Fig. 19-4. *Ollin meori* **hairstyle**

(Mural on the north wall of the burial chamber, Deokheung-ri Mural Tomb in Nampo, North K.orea)

Fig.19-5. *Naerin meori* **hairstyle**

(Mural on the northeast wall of the burial chamber, Gakjeochong in Ji'an, China)

Fig. 19-6. *Naerin meori* **hairstyle**

(Mural on the south wall of the first burial chamber, Samsilchong in Ji'an, China)

Fig. 20-1. Ankle-high leather shoes

(Mural on the north wall of the burial chamber, Suryeopchong in Nampo, North Korea)

Fig. 20-2. White shoes

(Mural on the north wall of the burial chamber, Deokheung-ri Mural Tomb in Nampo, North Korea)

Fig. 20-3. Shoes with gaiters

(Mural on the west wall of the burial chamber, Susan-ri Mural Tomb in Nampo, North Korea)

Fig. 20-4. Shoes with upturned tips

(Mural on the ceiling corbels of the burial chamber, Ohoebun Tomb No. 4 in Ji'an, China)

Fig. 21-1. Kitchen

(Mural on the east wall of the eastern side chamber attached to the antechamber, Anak Tomb No. 3 in Anak, North Korea)

Fig. 21-2. Earthenware steamer and iron kettle

(Guui-dong Fort in Seoul, Seoul National University Museum)

Fig. 22-1. Delivery of food tables (replica)

(Mural on the southeast wall of the burial chamber, Muyongchong in Ji'an, China)

The southeastern side of the drawing depicts servants bringing out food tables prepared in the kitchen.

Fig. 22-2. Setting out food tables for the tomb occupant and his wives (replica)

(Mural on the northeast wall of the burial chamber, Gakjeochong in Ji'an, China)

Fig. 23. Acrobatics

(Mural on the west wall of the burial chamber, Susan-ri Mural Tomb in Nampo, North Korea)

An acrobat wearing a narrow-sleeved jacket and tight pants juggles three poles and five balls. He looks up at the sky as he widens his stance, slightly bends his knees, and pushes his hips backwards. Another acrobat throws a many-spoked wheel into the air and rotates it; the third acrobat balances on wooden rods that are as tall as a man while performing a difficult feat with two small objects on his fingertips.

Fig. 24. Acrobatics (tracing)

(Mural on the east wall of antechamber, Palcheong-ri Mural Tomb in Daedong, North Korea)

In the midst of the parade on the antechamber's east wall, acrobats perform for the tomb occupant who rides in an ox-drawn carriage. The various acrobatics are accompanied by the music of the drums and wind instruments. Each acrobat's expression is serious as he performs such feats as walking on long rods, spinning items in the air, juggling balls and poles.

Fig. 25. Acrobatics

(Mural on the north wall of the antechamber, Jangcheon Tomb No. 1 in Ji'an, China)

Fig. 26. Dancing

(Mural on the north wall of the antechamber, Jangcheon Tomb No.1 in Ji'an, China)

This mural depicts dancers wearing long-sleeved jackets and white coronets attached by red straps, pentachord players powdering their faces and applying red lipstick and red rouge on their foreheads and cheeks with lotus flower buds, and female servants carrying pentachords.

Fig. 27. Dance with musical accompaniment (tracing)

(Mural on the west wall of the burial chamber, Anak Tomb No. 3 in Anak, North Korea)

A three-piece band and one dancer are portrayed. An apparently masked figure dances, crossing his legs in an x-shape and clapping to the accompaniment of the *piri* (Korean bamboo flute), *wanham* (Chinese lute-like instrument), and *geomungo* (Korean stringed musical instrument). If the dancer is in fact not masked, he can be interpreted as a figure from Central Asia, due to his prominent nose and facial appearance, which are atypical of Goguryeo people. For this reason, some think that the dancer is performing a dance that was popular in West and Central Asia.

Fig. 28. Dancing (tracing)

(Mural on the west wall of the burial chamber, southern chamber of Tonggu Tomb No. 12 in Ji'an, China)

Fig. 29. Dancing (replica)

(Mural on the southeast wall of the burial chamber, Muyongchong in Ji'an, China)

The northwestern side depicts household servants sending off their master with song and dance. This dancing scene is the reason the tomb is named "Muyongchong" (Tomb of the Dancers). The scene consists of the master departing on horseback, a page following him, and the dancers and the chorus-bidding farewell. The five dancers, who appear to be one straight line at first glance, are actually divided into one trio forming an oblique line and a right-hand pair standing parallel on a horizontal line. The painter's dynamic composition creates a sense of liveliness along with the alternating colors of the fourth and fifth dancers' *jeogori* and *baji* as well as the second and third dancers' topcoats of different hues. All the dancers hold the same posture, arms extended backward and appearing to sprout out from a single armpit. In contrast, the third figure in the group of seven presumed to be the chorus turns his head away from the tomb occupant.

Fig. 30. Dancing

(Corridor mural, eastern side of the burial chamber, Anak Tomb No. 3 in Anak, North Korea)

Fig. 31. *Geomungo*

(Mural on the ceiling corbels of the burial chamber, Muyongchong in Ji'an, China)

Fig. 32-1. *Wanham*

(Mural on the north wall of the antechamber, Deokheung-ri Mural Tomb in Nampo, North Korea)

Fig. 32-2. *Wanham*

(Mural on the ceiling corbels of the first burial chamber, Samsilchong in Ji'an, China)

Fig. 33-1. Horn trumpet

(Corridor mural, eastern side of the burial chamber, Anak Tomb No. 3 in Anak, North Korea)

Fig. 33-2. Horn trumpet

(Mural on the south wall of the antechamber, Deokheung-ri Mural Tomb in Nampo, North Korea)

Fig. 33-3. Horn trumpet

(Mural on the ceiling corbels of the first burial chamber, Samsilchong in Ji'an, China)

Fig. 34. *So*

(Corridor mural, eastern side of the burial chamber, Anak Tomb No. 3 in Anak, North Korea)

Fig. 35-1. Drum

(Corridor mural, eastern side of the burial chamber, Anak Tomb No. 3 in Anak, North Korea)

Fig. 35-2. Drum

(Mural on the south wall of the antechamber, Deokheung-ri Mural Tomb in Nampo, North Korea)

Fig. 35-3. Drum

(Mural on the east wall of the burial chamber, Susan-ri Mural Tomb in Nampo, North Korea)

Two men hoist a drum on their shoulders, while another man hits it. From the facial expressions of the front carrier who thrusts out his chest and throws his head back as the strap is placed on his shoulder, the combined weight of the drum, strap, and parasol must be heavy for even two men. The painter positioned the drummer behind the drum lest the beautiful patterns on the drum's surface be hidden. Only the drummer's shoes and narrow pants can be seen below the drum. The drum also hangs on hooks installed on the outside of the right and left stands, as perhaps the drum is too heavy to be carried only with the shoulder straps. Above the shoulder straps of the drum, a parasol provides shade.

Fig. 35-4. Janggu

(Mural on the ceiling corbels of the burial chamber, Ohoebun Tomb No. 4 in Ji'an, China)

Fig. 36. Gongs and bells

(Corridor mural, eastern side of the burial chamber, Anak Tomb No. 3 in Anak, North Korea)

Fig. 37. Marching band

(Corridor mural, eastern side of the burial chamber, Anak Tomb No. 3 in Anak, North Korea)

Each member of this 64-member marching band is painted with soft and refined brushstrokes and vivid colors. The musicians' movements and poses are depicted very realistically.

Fig. 38. Archery contest on horseback

(Mural on the west wall of the antechamber, Deokheung-ri Mural Tomb in Nampo, North Korea)

On the upper part of the west wall is painted a scene of *masahui* (馬射戲), a game in which mounted archers shoot an arrow at a target. At the bottom, a figure wearing black hemp headwear rides a horse and twists his torso to the rear as he aims his bow. The horseman on the right also pulls back his bow while above him another horseman awaits his turn. Standing among the horsemen are judges and scorekeepers. It appears that *masahui* was a very popular form of training and exercise in Goguryeo where great importance was attached to mounted archery.

Fig. 39-1. Hunting

(Mural on the ceiling corbels of the antechamber, Deokheung-ri Mural Tomb in Nampo, North Korea)

The upper part of the antechamber's eastern and western ceiling corbels depicts the heavenly world, while the lower part shows a hunting ground. In the heavenly world are mythical flying fish, two-headed bird, heavenly horse, and phoenix centering on the sun in which a three-legged crow is. A winged fish flies in the sky and a phoenix steps on a fire with its feet. On the hunting ground, horsemen ride across a mountain and aim their bows at the necks of deer or tigers. Though surrounded already by the hunters, a wild boar and a roe deer flee for shelter. Two men in black hemp headwear attempt to aim their bows again at a tiger already wounded by an arrow in its neck. A deer pierced by an arrow lifts up its front legs as if surprised. The mountains and trees are represented to be smaller than the hunters and animals and painted as if cut out of a paperboard. An unrealistically posed hunter, with his head turned over his shoulder as in Parthian-style archery, catches the eye.

Fig. 39-2. Hunting

(Mural on the west and south walls of the antechamber, Yaksu-ri Mural Tomb in Nampo, North Korea)

A large-scale hunting scene is painted in the space extending from the south wall of the antechamber to the west wall. However, details are difficult to distinguish as a considerable portion of the mural's northern end has deteriorated. Nonetheless, the remaining portions reveal vivid depictions of mounted figures pursuing a tiger, a deer, and other animals, archers, beaters flushing out animals from a mountain, and horsemen rushing to a hunting ground. On the right, figures appear to try to stir up excitement by beating drums and blowing horns. This is a good example of the large-scale hunting practiced in Goguryeo. Below the picture can be seen a stable and a procession of figures.

Fig. 39-3. Hunting (replica)

(Mural on the northwest wall of the burial chamber, Muyongchong in Ji'an, China)

A hunting scene is on the left and two ox-drawn carriages on the right. A large tree acts as the border between the two scenes. With powerful, concise strokes, the mural captures the tension-filled chase as hunters pursue fleeing animals. The thick and thin undulating lines of the mountain provide a sense of speed and tension to the deer, tigers and the men on horseback who ride facing forward or turning backward as they aim their bows. Whereas the stance and motion of the men and animals are expressed with relative accuracy and sophistication, the mountains and water are portrayed in a rudimentary fashion, with the mountain ridges lacking spatial sense and the trees on the mountain peaks resembling bracken sprouts. Despite the absence of perspective and the unproportionate sizes, the artificially depicted elements of mountains, men, animals and trees all meld into a fluid, elegant feeling of motion.

Fig. 39-4. Hunting with falconry

(Mural on the south wall of the first burial chamber, Samsilchong in Ji'an, China)

Fig. 39-5. Hunting with falconry

(Mural on the north wall of the antechamber, Jangcheon Tomb No. 1 in Ji'an,

China)

Fig. 40-1. *Ssireum*

(Mural on the southeast wall of the burial chamber, Gakjeochong in Ji'an, China)

A large tree in the center divides the mural, with a kitchen scene on the left and a *ssireum* scene on the right that is one of the oldest pictorial representations of the Korean form of wrestling. The tightened lines of the *ssireum* athletes' arm and leg muscles create a sense of tense competition. An old man holding a cane appears to be refereeing the *ssireum* competition. When the mural was first examined in the 1930s, the two *ssireum* athletes were in relatively good condition but now the torso of the Goguryeo *ssireum* athlete and the lower legs of the Western *ssireum* athlete have been badly damaged. Black birds on the branches of the purple tree and a bear and a tiger on either side of the tree's base are animals related to the traditional faith of the Goguryeo people. In addition, the animals' poses and facial expressions are vivid examples of the early stage of genre painting.

Fig. 40-2. *Ssireum*

(Mural on the north wall of the antechamber, Jangcheon Tomb No. 1 in Ji'an, China)

Fig. 40-3. *Subak*

(Mural on the east wall of the antechamber, Anak Tomb No. 3 in Anak, North Korea)

Subak (手搏) is a form of unarmed martial art popular in the ancient East Asia. In Goguryeo, ordinary soldiers who excelled at *subak* were promoted as officials. Unlike the *subak* scene on the Muyongchong mural, the arms and feet of fighters on the Anak Tomb No. 3 mural are drawn less clearly, with softer brush lines, thus failing to create either suspense or verisimilitude. Also noteworthy is that one of the fighters is portrayed with large, Western eyes and an aquiline nose, as in the Muyongchong mural.

Fig. 40-4. *Subak*

(Mural on the ceiling corbels of the burial chamber, Muyongchong in Ji'an, China)

Two nearly naked fighters, one with typical Goguryeo features and one with Western facial characteristics, wear topknots while taking a sparring posture from a form of martial arts called *taekgyeon*. Power and tension emanate from their flexed or taut upper and lower limbs.

Fig. 41-1. Ox-drawn carriage

(Corridor mural, eastern side of the burial chamber, Anak Tomb No. 3 in Anak, North Korea)

Fig. 41-2. Ox-drawn carriage

(Mural on the east wall of the passage, Deokheung-ri Mural Tomb in Nampo, North Korea)

This is a procession for the tomb occupant's wife. Female servants line up on both sides of the covered carriage in which she rides. Women with their hair in chignons are drawn larger than young girls with their hair braided into pigtails. All the servants are dressed in long *jeogori* (jacket) and *jureum chima* (pleated skirt), under which can be seen the bottoms of their pants; these outfits are helpful in understanding women's clothing in early fifth-century Goguryeo.

Fig. 41-3. Ox-drawn carriage

(Mural on the northwest wall of the burial chamber, Muyongchong in Ji'an, China)

Fig. 42. God of the sun and goddess of the moon

(Mural on the ceiling corbels of the burial chamber, Ohoebun Tomb No. 4 in Ji'an, China)

On the triangular stones in the north corner of the ceiling corbels are drawn the god of the sun and the goddess of the moon. With his hair hanging loose, the god of the sun raises his hands above his head to support the round sun in which lies a three-legged crow. While the god of the sun's upper half is human, his lower half is that of a dragon. He wears blue wings with yellow feathers and extends his legs in the front and back. The goddess of the moon has a white face and red lips. With her long hair fluttering, she holds the round moon above her head. A toad lies at the moon's center. Like the god of the sun, she is half-human and half-dragon, with her lower half shining in five colors. She looks as if in mid-leap, one foot stretched forward and the other backwards, creating a strong sense of motion.

Fig. 43. Heaven

(Mural on the ceiling corbels of the burial chamber, Ohoebun Tomb No. 5 in Ji'an, China)

Painted on the burial chamber's ceiling corbels are heavenly orbs and constellations including the sun, the moon and the Big Dipper, cloud patterns, various gods of civilization, heavenly beings, and auspicious animals. Each level of the corbels features two immortals riding on auspicious animals while playing musical instruments such as the *bipa*, Korean lutes, flutes, and the *janggu* (hourglass-shaped drum). On a corner of the triangular corbel, a dragon supports the world of heaven and on the sides of the corbels are various gods including the god of the sun and the goddess of the moon and trees.

Fig. 44-1. God of war

(Mural on the ceiling corbels of the second burial chamber, Samsilchong in Ji'an, China)

Fig. 44-2. Gods of fire and agriculture

(Mural on the ceiling corbels of the burial chamber, Ohoebun Tomb No. 4 in Ji'an, China)

The god of fire is bareheaded with loose hair. As he looks at the torch in his right hand that is stretched behind his back, he appears as if he is dancing. The god of agriculture has a cow's head and runs forward with his arms spread wide, holding some ears of grains in his right hand.

Fig. 45-1. God of blacksmiths

(Mural on the ceiling corbels of the burial chamber, Ohoebun Tomb No. 5 in Ji'an, China)

In this mural, the god of blacksmiths hammers on a lump of steel as he steadies it with fire tongs on an anvil.

Fig. 45-2. God of the wheel

(Mural on the ceiling corbels of the burial chamber, Ohoebun Tomb No. 4 in Ji'an, China)

The god of the wheel inspects a cartwheel, hitting it with a hammer.

Fig. 45-3. God of whetstone

(Mural on the ceiling corbels of the burial chamber, Ohoebun Tomb No. 5 in Ji'an, China)

Wearing leather shoes with upturned tips, the god refines and crafts useful tools of civilization.

Fig. 46-1. Immortal

(Mural on the ceiling corbels of the burial chamber, Ohoebun Tomb No. 4 in Ji'an, China)

Wearing a white coronet and black clothing with a yellow collar, an immortal rides a crane.

Fig. 46-2. Immortals

(Mural on the ceiling corbels of the burial chamber, Ohoebun Tomb No. 4 in Ji'an, China)

On the eastern side of the ceiling corbels, an immortal blows a bamboo flute while riding on an auspicious bird and another immortal grasps a banner while riding on a dragon. The sky seems filled with the sounds of the bamboo flute. Both immortals wear clothes with trim, a characteristic of Goguryeo costumes.

Fig. 47. Immortal (replica)

(Mural on the ceiling corbels of the burial chamber, Muyongchong in Ji'an, China)

An immortal with an especially long neck and animal ears is blowing a long horn. Several beams of auspicious energy project from the sharply split sleeves and pants. This depiction of immortals was popular in fifth-century Goguryeo.

Fig. 48. Heaven

(Mural on the ceiling corbels of the antechamber, Deokheung-ri Mural Tomb in Nampo, North Korea)

The ceiling corbels of the antechamber in the Deokheung-ri Mural Tomb reveal which vivid legends and narratives about the heavenly world predominated in the minds of the Goguryeo people. Although there are some beings whose cultural lineage and origin are obscure, the sun, the moon, constellations and other heavenly beings are sufficient material to understand the diversity of Northeast Asian cultures, including Goguryeo, up to the early fifth century. Inscriptions beside each strange animal such as *cheonjak* (天雀), *jichuk* (地軸), *cheonma* (天馬), *yeongyang* (零陽), *byeokdok* (辟毒), *hwewon* (喙遠), *hajo* (賀鳥), *bagwi* (博位), etc. help, to explicate the views of heaven and universe in the fifth century. The heavenly world in Goguryeo murals is an ideal world where immortals, sacred birds, and animals frolic. On the west ceiling corbels are painted the moon, several constellations, immortals and Ongnyeo, *cheonchu*, *manse*, and the like. An immortal flies to the left, holding a *dang* (幢 banner) in his left hand; and Ongnyeo follows him, holding a *beon* (幡 standard) in her left hand. Underneath, another Ongnyeo flies in the same direction and holds *ban* (盤 tray). Birds named *cheonchu* and *manse* with human heads, created by the desire for longevity, also appear.

Fig. 49-1. Mythical bird *cheonchu*

(Mural on the ceiling corbels of the burial chamber, Muyongchong in Ji'an, China)

Fig. 49-2. Mythical bird *cheonchu*

(Mural on the ceiling corbels of the second burial chamber, Samsilchong in

Ji'an, China)

Fig. 49-3. Mythical bird *manse*
(Mural on the ceiling corbels of the antechamber, Deokheung-ri Mural Tomb in Nampo, North Korea)

Fig. 50-1. *Girin*
(Mural on the ceiling corbels of the burial chamber, Anak Tomb No. 1 in Anak, North Korea)

Fig. 50-2. *Girin*
(Mural on the ceiling corbels of the burial chamber, Muyongchong in Ji'an, China)

Fig. 50-3. *Girin*
(Mural on the ceiling corbels of the second burial chamber, Samsilchong in Ji'an, China)

Fig. 50-4. *Girin*
(Mural on the ceiling corbels of the burial chamber, Gangseodaemyo in Pyeongyang, North Korea)

Fig. 51-1. Mythical bird *yangsu*
(Mural on the ceiling corbels of the burial chamber, Deokheung-ri Mural Tomb in Nampo, North Korea)
Beside two lines of Chinese characters, "陽邃之鳥 履火而行," a bird spreads its wings and opens its beak to cry out loud. As indicated by the inscription,

the bird stepping on a fire is a phoenix.

Fig. 51-2. Mythical bird

(Mural on the ceiling corbels of the burial chamber, Gangseodaemyo in Pyeongyang, North Korea)

Fig. 51-3. Man-headed animal

(Mural on the ceiling corbels of the burial chamber, Anak Tomb No. 1 in Anak, North Korea)

The beast has a human head, but unfortunately only a portion of the head has been preserved from deterioration, making it difficult to identify details. The body of the beast resembles that of *seongseong* in the Deokheung-ri Mural Tomb.

Fig. 51-4. Heavenly deer *cheollok*

(Mural on the ceiling corbels of the second burial chamber, Samsilchong in Ji'an, China)

Fig. 51-5. Heavenly horse *cheonma*

(Mural on the ceiling corbels of the burial chamber, Deokheung-ri Mural Tomb in Nampo, North Korea)

Fig. 51-6. Mythical flying fish *bieo*

(Mural on the ceiling corbels of the antechamber, Deokheung-ri Mural Tomb in Nampo, North Korea)

Fig. 51-7. Heavenly horse *cheonma* and mythical flying fish *bieo*

(Mural on the ceiling corbels of the burial chamber, Anak Tomb No. 1 in

Anak, North Korea)

Bieo (飛魚 flying fish) and *cheonma* (天馬 heavenly horse) are depicted on the
second level of the ceiling corbels and are among the strange birds and beasts
that appear in the *Shanhaijing* (山海經). The beasts of Anak Tomb No. 1,
including the heavenly horse, are characterized by wings on their shoulders,
in contrast to the wingless heavenly horse painted on the antechamber ceiling
of the Deokheung-ri Mural Tomb. The mythical flying fish of the
Deokheung-ri mural is similar to that of Anak Tomb No. 1 as well.

Fig. 52. Procession for worship to Buddha

(Mural on the west wall of the burial chamber, Ssangyeongchong in Nampo,
North Korea)

Part of a procession decorating the west wall of the burial chamber, the mural
still exhibits the methods of hierarchical expression which reflect the status and
position of a figure through size, though not to the same extent as the murals
from the early fifth century. In the procession, servants and noblewomen are
differentiated by size as well as attire. As the noblewoman wears a finely
pleated skirt and a long jacket with ornately patterned red trim, she can be
distinguished from other figures of the procession by costume as well as size.
A female servant wearing a dotted jacket and pants has her hair loose and
unornamented down her back like an unmarried girl. Walking behind the
noblewoman, the servant turns her head back with an expression as if she is
speaking to someone behind her. A page wearing a sleeveless jacket and pants
appears to be listening to the servant at the rear of the procession.

Fig. 53-1. Rites offered before a statue of Buddha

(Mural on the ceiling corbels of the antechamber, Jangcheon Tomb No. 1 in

Ji'an, China)

At the center of the painting, a Tathagata sits cross-legged on a pedestal (*sumijwa* 須彌座) his hands in a mudra of concentration, left hand placed on the right hand and resting on the abdomen. An incense burner is carved in the middle of the pedestal, with guardian animals on either side. To the left stand a noble and his wife who came to offer a memorial service. To their rear, two female servants wait with white towels laid on their left shoulders. An image of male and female children being born from a lotus flower appears behind the servants. On the right side are two worshippers who appear to be husband and wife; the two have approached the Tathagata and are kneeling, prostrated with their heads and arms against the floor (五體投地). On the upper part of the painting are haloed *bicheon* (飛天 *apsara*). Lotus flower buds fill the spaces between the human figures offering memorial services to the Tathagata. Precious jewels, a red phoenix and a *girin* are painted on the lower part of the mural. Each layer of the ceiling corbels is populated with bodhisattvas and beings from the Buddhist paradise such as lotus flowers and *apsaras*.

Fig. 53-2. Bodhisattvas and *apsaras*

(Mural on the ceiling corbels of the antechamber, Jangcheon Tomb No. 1 in Ji'an, China)

Bodhisattvas and *apsaras* are depicted on the left and right sides of the memorial service mural, but, unfortunately the southern bodhisattvas are unidentifiable in sections of the faces and costumes due to fading or disintegrating lime. The bodhisattvas stand on lotus pedestals (蓮臺) facing the Tathagata. Their faces are clean-shaven or bearded and they wear coronets with halos behind their heads. At either end are depictions of the lotus flower births of children with boys' faces; again only portions can be observed due to deterioration of the mural. Above the bodhisattvas, *apsaras* fly toward precious jewels drawn slightly below the mid-point. All of them wear topknots, halos, and long pants, but are barefooted and bare-chested.

Fig. 53-3. *Sanhwa gongyang*

(Mural on the ceiling corbels of the burial chamber, Anak Tomb No. 2 in Anak, North Korea)

A *bicheon* (*apsara*) flies in the air, holding up a dish with lotus leaves for *sanhwa gongyang* (散花供養). The lower edges of the *apsara*'s garments flutter in flight.

Fig. 54-1. Ceiling filled with lotuses

(Mural on the ceiling corbels of the burial chamber, Anak Tomb No. 2 in Anak, North Korea)

The ceiling corbels of this burial chamber is the literal depiction of *yeonhwa jeongto* (蓮花淨土 lotus flower paradise) of Buddhism. The side and base of each ceiling and ceiling stone are all decorated with lotuses or lotus-related patterns. It can be conjectured that the tomb occupant's ultimate hope for his future life is the Buddhist paradise.

Fig. 54-2. Lotus, the sun, and the moon

(Mural on the ceiling corbels of the burial chamber, Ssangyeongchong in Nampo, North Korea)

A lotus in full bloom is painted in the center of the ceiling stone. Flows of strong force are represented on the bases of the second level of the *samgak goim* (triangular corbels) as well as the bases of the first level of the south and north triangular corbels. The sun and the moon drawn on the bases of the first level of the east and west triangular corbels. The lotus on the ceiling stone has eight, five-layered petals. While the outer petal ends are pointed, the petal lobe is a gentle, round arc; and the leaf's veins are represented, but a stamen and a pistil are omitted. Furthermore, the ovary is narrowed, the inner round petals reduced, and bead patterns within the inner petal omitted. This is not characteristic of fifth century Ji'an and Pyeongyang-style paintings, and perhaps results from the synthesization of the two lotus representation methods. The crest of the three-legged crow within the sun is tightly rolled up like a butterfly's antenna, and the end of its folded wing is flung outwards. The toad in the moon, which lies on its belly, belches flame as it turns its head toward the left. Although the degree of realistic portrayal differs significantly, the shape of the toad's head recalls the tortoise head of black tortoise-snakes seen in Four Directional Deities tomb murals from the sixth and seventh centuries. This representation of the toad within the moon is not found in other Goguryeo murals.

Fig. 55. Lotus in the ceiling stone

(Mural on the ceiling corbels of the burial chamber, Anak Tomb No. 3 in Anak, North Korea)

A lotus in full bloom is portrayed in the center of the ceiling stone. The lotus has eight, two-layered petals for a total of 16 petals; and the petal's outer part is wide with the ends tapered. Five pistils and stamens create a naturalistic impression. Considering characteristics such as the double arc of the petal's outer part, the symmetrical lines drawn on the petals and the flower as a whole, the shape of petals formed by the unnatural contact of straight lines and crescent-shaped lines, and so forth, we can see a correlation between this lotus and the lotus patterns of Korean roof-end tiles in the fourth century.

Fig. 56-1. Lotus

(Mural on the ceiling corbels of the burial chamber, Jinpa-ri Tomb No. 4 in Pyeongyang, North Korea)

The bases of the triangular corbels of the burial chamber are decorated with honeysuckle leaves and fully-blossomed lotus flowers. The eight, two-layered petals are peach-shaped with bead-like pistils and wide ovaries. As the honeysuckle leaves are more static and smaller compared to the flowers, they seem more stylized compared to the lotus flowers on the parallel corbels.

Fig. 56-2. Birth from a lotus flower

(Mural on the north wall of the burial chamber, Jinpari Tomb No. 1 in Pyeongyang, North Korea)

Fig. 57-1. Birth from a lotus flower

(Mural on the ceiling corbels of the burial chamber, Muyongchong in Ji'an, China)

On the first level of the *pyeonghaeng goim* (parallel corbels) adjacent to the burial chamber are successive triangular flame patterns; on the second level, lotus flower buds and lotus flowers rise to the sky. This mural is reminiscent of the Buddhist belief that people can be reborn in paradise as lotus flowers.

Fig. 57-2. Birth from a lotus flower

(Mural on the ceiling corbels of the second burial chamber, Samsilchong in Ji'an, China)

Fig. 57-3. Birth from a lotus flower

(Mural on the ceiling corbels of the second burial chamber, Samsilchong in

Ji'an, China)

Fig. 57-4. Birth from a lotus flower

(Mural on the ceiling corbels of the antechamber, Jangcheon Tomb No. 1 in Ji'an, China)

Fig. 57-5. Birth from a lotus flower

(Mural on the north wall of the burial chamber, Jinpa-ri Tomb No. 1 in Pyeongyang, North Korea)

Fig. 57-6. Lotus pond

(Mural on the southern part of the east wall of the entrance passage, Jinpa-ri Tomb No. 4 in Pyeongyang, North Korea)

On the east and west walls are the heavenly ponds of *yeonhwa jeongto* (lotus paradise). In a Buddhist paradise, the pond spreads between a rocky mountain and woods full of reflections from precious jewels. On the pond's southern end, a lotus stalk rises between wind-blown waves; lotus buds open; honeysuckle spreads to the right and left of the lotuses; and auspicious energies extend above them. Several evergreen trees rise between awe-inspiring rocks and cliffs. The honeysuckle leaves sprouting out of the soaring lotus buds indicate that the lotus buds originate from the Buddhist paradise.

Yeonhwa jeongto is the nest of the heavenly lotus that gives rebirth to all beings. The lotuses flying in the air above the pond are beings that will be reborn as other creatures of the *yeonhwa jeongto* world. This mural is one of the extant concrete depictions of the Goguryeo people's faith in *cheonsuguk* (天壽國, paradise).

Fig. 58. A jewel born from lotus

(Mural on the ceiling corbels of the burial chamber, Gangseodaemyo in Nampo, North Korea)

Fig. 59-1. Constellations

(Mural on the ceiling stone of the burial chamber, Jinpa-ri Tomb No. 4 in Pyeongyang, North Korea)

Honeysuckle patterns are painted on the first level of the parallel corbels; on the second level, *byeongpung* (folding-screen) patterns; and checkered ring and honeysuckle vine patterns are on the first level of triangular corbels. On the ceiling stone, over 91 stars and constellations including 28 constellations along the ecliptic were painted in gold dust. This mural can be considered evidence of the origin of Goguryeo astronomy, which culminated in a stone astronomical chart that featured 1,467 stars and 238 constellations that is said to have been thrown into the Daedonggang river when Goguryeo was destroyed. Most of the gold dust has fallen from the ceiling stone and at present, only vestiges remain. Honeysuckle and lotuses are depicted on the base of the triangular corbel.

Fig. 59-2. Four Directional Deities and the 28 constellations

(Kim, Il-kwon)

Fig. 60-1. Cheongnyong (Blue Dragon)

(Mural on the east wall of the burial chamber, Yaksu-ri Mural Tomb in Nampo, North Korea)

At the top of the burial chamber's east wall, the Cheongnyong (青龍) is painted along with the sun in which a three-legged crow lies and constellations presumed to be Bangsu (房宿) and Gaksu (角宿) which consist of three stars and two stars, respectively. As the dragon's neck, body, tail and legs are the same thickness, a sense of volume as an animal is negligible; this may be due to a still developing conception of the Four Directional Deities.

Fig. 60-2. Baekho (White Tiger)

(Mural on the west wall of the burial chamber, Yaksu-ri Mural Tomb in Nampo, North Korea)

This painting exhibits symmetry with the Cheongnyong, the sun, and constellations on the east wall. At the top of the west wall, the Baekho (白虎) is painted with the moon, constellations presumed to be Samsu (參宿) and Jasu (觜宿) which consist of three stars and two stars, respectively, and several deformed cloud patterns. The tiger is posed as if treading on a crossbeam, and like the dragon, every part of its body is of the same thickness. The tiger's facial expression is notable for its naturalistic characteristics such as the wave-patterned stripes on the body, triangular ears, and round tip nose, etc. The moon is shown as a red circle on which a toad is painted.

Fig. 60-3. Jujak (Red Phoenix)

(Mural on the south wall of the burial chamber, Yaksu-ri Mural Tomb in Nampo, North Korea)

The Jujak (朱雀), located at the top of the south wall above the burial chamber's door, is painted together with Myosu (昴宿), a constellation that symbolizes the south. The awkwardness of its legs and facial features — the crest, beak, and eyes — may be attributed to the painter's attempt to be faithful to the literal description of Jujak. It holds between its teeth the *sadang* fruit which a phoenix is said to hold when crossing Yaksu (弱水).

Fig. 60-4. Hyeongmu (Black Tortoise-Serpent)

(Mural on the north wall of the burial chamber, Yakusu-ri Mural Tomb in Nampo, North Korea)

Above a crossbeam at the top of the north wall are painted the tomb occupant, his wife, and the Hyeonmu (玄武). The tomb occupant and his wife are seated on a *pyeongsang* (flat bench) in a curtained room, being waited upon by servants; the Hyeonmu stands outside of the room, to the right of the picture. To show difference in status, the servants are drawn smaller than the aristocratic couple. Around the Hyeonmu and the couple are deformed cloud patterns; and above them, the Big Dipper and Jingnyeosu (織女宿). As for the tortoise, its body is decorated with tortoise shell patterns, but, in fact, its shape is that of a wild animal like a dog, revealing how the Hyeonmu was considered as a being that safeguards the tomb owner and his wife.

Fig. 61-1. Cheongnyong

(Mural on the east wall of the burial chamber, Honam-ri Sasinchong in Pyeongyang, North Korea)

The Cheongnyong stands with its head turned, watching its own tail. The face and shape of the head are similar to the Cheongnyong of Deokhwa-ri Tomb No. 1 and Deokhwa-ri Tomb No. 2 murals; however, it differs in that it has a single horn, no exaggerated eyebrows, and no *cheongmok* (尺木), considered necessary for flight, behind the neck. Strong flame-shaped force lines emanating from the shoulder joint appear to be leather wings at first glance. Also as its tail does not stretch backward, but is instead depicted in inverse-tiered style, this Cheongnyong deviates from the examples in other tomb murals.

Fig. 61-2. Cheongnyong

(Mural on the east wall of the burial chamber, Gangseodaemyo in Nampo, North Korea)

The Cheongnyong appears as if it is about to head south with its left front foot advancing far forward. Flame-shaped wing feathers project from the shoulder and thin hairs sprout from the back of the legs. The features — Cheongnyong's thin neck and thick trunk which from a large "S" shape, the flexibly projected tail shaped like stairs and the four legs appropriately extended forwards and backwards — harmonize together to create a natural yet powerful Cheongnyong. Development in the depiction of Four Directional Deities from earlier ancient tomb wall paintings can be seen in the following: large eyes that appear on the verge of popping out, the red tongue thrust out, the large ears and the two thin horns projected upward. On the back of the neck are flame-shaped scaled processes and below the neck is a white and red three-colored band. The splendid coloring and details are eye-catching.

Fig. 61-3. Baekho

(Mural on the west wall of the burial chamber, Honam-ri Sasinchong in Pyeongyang, North Korea)

Similar to the Cheongnyong on the east wall, the Baekho also stands with its head turned watching its tail. The Baekho's head is shaped like a natural tiger. However, from the unrealistic portrayal of the Baekho's face, such as the representation of the opposite eye and ear which should not be seen from the lateral side, we can surmise that this is a transitional depiction shifting to the more characteristic Four Directional Deities mural.

Fig. 61-4. Baekho

(Mural on the west wall of the burial chamber, Gangseodaemyo in Nampo, North Korea)

The Baekho appears to run toward the entrance of burial chamber, its mouth open to roar. While the Baekho's basic posture closely resembles that of the Cheongnyong on the east wall, differing only in the steeper inverted S-curve of the neck line, the less detailed trunk and the thinner legs, these small details create the tiger's distinctive mood. As in the Cheongnyong painting, a white and red three-colored band encircles the body below its neck.

Fig. 61-5, 6. Jujak

(Mural on the south wall of the burial chamber, Honam-ri Sasinchong in Pyeongyang, North Korea)

On the south wall, the Jujak stand spreading their wings opposite on another with the door of the burial chamber between them. Unlike the Jujak in other tomb murals, these have neither special feather ornaments on their crowns nor exaggerated beaks, and their tail feathers are relatively simple. A further peculiarity is that while the outside wing's feathers are long like those of a crane, the inside wing's feathers are relatively uniform like those of non-migratory birds. The lack of feather decoration on the Jujak's crown is similar to the representation of the Jujak among Four Directional Deities carved on metal coffin decorations unearthed from Oya-ri Tomb No. 19 in the district of Nangnang, Pyeongyang.

Fig. 61-7, 8. Jujak

(Mural on the south wall of the burial chamber, Gangseodaemyo in Nampo, North Korea)

The Jujak look at the entrance of the burial chamber with widely spread wings that almost form a circle. The birds' characteristics—the wide eyes, head feathers stretched far backward, neck and body constituting an "S" shape, fully spread wings, three-stranded tail feathers forcefully elevated and the threateningly lifted one leg—create a fierce and powerful Jujak. In their beaks, both hold strands of lotus flower buds wrapped in luxuriant honeysuckle leaves. On their necks are two lines of colored bands and below their legs are mountains and rocks.

Fig. 61-9. Hyeonmu

(Mural on the north wall of the burial chamber, Honam-ri Sasinchong in Pyeongyang, North Korea)

On the north wall, the Hyeonmu is depicted in such a way that the snake coils around the tortoise's body three times from the front to the rear, then lifts its body upward, and pulls back its neck in the form of a reverse "S," looking at the front of the tortoise. The tortoise is looking up, lifting its head. Thus, in this mural, the serpent and the tortoise are not looking at each other. Such a pose is not found in other tomb murals, and does not agree with the principle of Hyeonmu representation, in which female *yin* and male *yang* are in concert with each other.

Fig. 61-10. Hyeonmu

(Mural on the north wall of the burial chamber, Gangseodaemyo in Nampo, North Korea)

On the north wall, the Hyeonmu heads west. The serpent loops between the tortoise's back legs to coil once around the shell, then passes between the two front legs to make a half-circle, winds around the front of the tortoise's neck, and then loops its own tail to face the tortoise. From the widely opened mouths of the tortoise and the serpent gush *yin* and *yang* energies like flames. The two energies meet each other at the apex of the triangle, thereby achieving harmony between *yin* and *yang* and the reproduction of the universe's order, i.e., the purpose of the Hyeonmu's existence. As the tortoise's motion and the snake's elasticity combine into one, the Hyeonmu in the mural is reborn as a mysterious being that discharges the energy of the universe.

Fig. 61-11. Hwangnyong (Yellow Dragon)

(Mural on the ceiling stone of the burial chamber, Gangseodaemyo in Nampo, North Korea)

In the course of a tomb robbery, the ceiling stone of the burial chamber of Gangseodaemyo was broken into three pieces. A fully blossomed lotus is drawn on each of the four corners of the ceiling stone. In the stone's center is a figure of a coiled Hwangnyong about to spring forth. Flows of strong energies are depicted around the dragon. On the bases of the second level of the triangular corbel just below the ceiling stone, lotus flowers and honeysuckle leaves are drawn in each corner. On the bases of the first level of the triangular corbel, honeysuckle and lotus flowers are drawn in the same manner except for the addition of two auspicious birds that face each other with their wings flapping. In the spaces adjacent to the base of the parallel corbel are three honeysuckle lotus flowers in full blossom.

Fig. 62-1. Sun and moon

(Mural on the ceiling stone of the burial chamber, Jinpa-ri Tomb No.1 in Nampo, North Korea)

Fig. 62-2. Sun

(Mural on the ceiling corbels of the burial chamber, Gakjeochong in Ji'an, China)

Fig. 62-3. Sun

(Mural on the ceiling corbels of the burial chamber, Ssangyeongchong in Nampo, North Korea)

Fig. 62-4. Sun

(Mural on the ceiling corbels of the burial chamber, Ohoebun Tomb No. 4 in Ji'an, China)

Fig. 62-5. Moon

(Mural on the ceiling corbels of the antechamber, Deokheung-ri Mural Tomb in Nampo, North Korea)

Fig. 62-6. Moon

(Mural on the ceiling corbels of the burial chamber, Ssangyeongchong in Nampo, North Korea)

Fig. 62-7. Moon

(Mural on the ceiling corbels of the burial chamber, Deokhwa-ri Tomb No. 1 in Daedong, North Korea)

Fig. 63. Sun, moon, Big Dipper

(Mural on the ceiling corbels of the burial chamber, Jangcheon Tomb No. 1 in Ji'an, China)

Next to the inscription of the Chinese characters "北斗七青," the Big Dipper and the Namdu Six Stars (Milk Dipper) are painted on the ceiling stone along with the sun with a three-legged crow inside and the moon with a rabbit and a toad drawn inside. The constellations are arranged inside small circles and the stars connected to each other by straight lines.

Fig. 64. Big Dipper

(Mural on the ceiling corbels of the burial chamber, Deokhwa-ri Tomb No. 1 in Daedong, North Korea)

Fig. 65. Big Dipper and earth axis

(Mural on the ceiling corbels of the antechamber, Deokheung-ri Mural Tomb in Nampo, North Korea)

Underneath the Big Dipper stands a four-legged beast with human heads at both ends of its body; and on the left the Chinese characters "地軸一身兩頭" are written inside a yellow strip, from which it can be inferred that the central axis which fixes the earth in place has been given the shape of a human head. This is the same basic shape as that painted on the burial chamber's ceiling of Cheonwangjisinchong in Suncheon.

Fig. 66-1. Sanseongha Tombs in Ji'an, China

Fig. 66-2. Cheonchuchong in Ji'an, China

Fig. 66-3. Jechong of Sanseongha Tombs in Ji'an, China

Fig. 67-1. Janggunchong in Ji'an , China (1920s)

Fig. 67-2. Janggunchong in Ji'an, China (2007)

Fig. 68-1. Anak Tomb No. 3 in Anak, North Korea

Fig. 68-2. The interior of Anak Tomb No. 3 in Anak, North Korea

Fig. 68-3. Janggun Tomb of Michanggu Tombs in Huanren, China

Fig. 68-4. The interior of Janggun Tomb of Michanggu Tombs in Huanren (replica)
(Liaoning Provincial Museum, China)

Fig. 68-5. Mausoleum of King Dongmyeong the Great in Pyeongyang, North Korea

Fig. 69-1. Gangseodaemyo in Nampo, North Korea

Fig. 69-2. Perspective view of the interior of Gangseodaemyo in Nampo, North Korea

Fig. 70. Passage of Taeseong-ri Tomb No. 3 in Nampo, North Korea

Fig. 71-1. Floor plan of the understructure of the Deokheung-ri

Mural Tomb in Nampo, North Korea

Fig. 71-2. Floor plan of the understructure of Gakjeochong in Ji'an, China

Fig. 72. Floor plan of the understructure of Deokhwa-ri Tomb No. 1 in Daedong, North Korea

Fig. 73. Floor plan of the understructure of Maseongu Tomb No. 1 in Ji' an, China

Fig. 74. Traditional fireplace plastered with lime mortar
(Maseongu Tomb No. 1 in Ji'an, China)

Fig. 75-1. Onyeo Mountain Fortress in Huanren, China

Fig. 75-2. Hwando Mountain Fortress in Ji'an, China

Fig. 75-3. Daeseong Mountain Fortress in Pyeongyang, North Korea

Fig. 76-1. Gungnaeseong Fortress in Ji'an, China

Fig. 76-2. Pyeongyangseong Fortress in Pyeongyang, North Korea

Fig. 77. *Chi* of Baegamseong Fortress in Dungta, China

Fig. 78. Headquarters of Baegamseong Fortress in Dungta, China

Fig. 79. Secret gate of Pyeongyangseong Fortress in Pyeongyang, North Korea

Fig. 80-1. Chart of Yodongseong Fortress (tracing)
(Mural on the south wall of the antechamber, Yodongseongchong in Suncheon, North Korea)

Fig. 80-2. Fortress chart (tracing)
(Mural on the south wall of the antechamber, Yonggangdaemyo in Nampo, North Korea)

Fig. 81. Fortress stone from Pyeongyangseong Fortress in Pyeongyang, North Korea

Fig. 82-1. Archer
(Corridor mural, eastern side of the burial chamber, Anak Tomb No. 3 in Anak, North Korea)

Fig. 82-2. Hunter
(Mural on the northwest wall of the burial chamber, Muyongchong in Ji'an, China)

Fig. 83-1. Warrior with spear
(Corridor mural, eastern side of the burial chamber, Anak Tomb No. 3 in Anak, North Korea)

Fig. 83-2. Warrior with spear

(Mural on the south wall of the burial chamber, Anak Tomb No. 2 in Anak, North Korea)

Defending the tomb occupant's resting place, armored warriors stand at the eastern and western sides of the southern entrance to the burial chamber. Both are in scale armor and helmets; the gatekeeper on the east wall holds a long spear and the gatekeeper on the west wall is poised to draw his sword called *hwandudaedo* (環頭大刀).

Fig. 83-3. Spear

(Guui-dong Fort in Seoul, Seoul National University Museum)

Fig. 83-4. Warrior with sword

(Corridor mural, eastern side of the burial chamber, Anak Tomb No. 3 in Anak, North Korea)

Fig. 83-5. Warrior with sword

(Mural on the west wall of the second burial chamber, Samsilchong in Ji'an China)

Fig. 83-6. Sword

(Guui-dong Fort in Seoul, Seoul National University Museum)

Fig. 83-7. Battle-ax warriors

(Corridor mural, eastern side of the burial chamber, Anak Tomb No. 3 in Anak, North Korea)

Fig. 83-8. Battle-ax warriors

(Mural on the east wall of the antechamber, Anak Tomb No. 3 in Anak, North

Korea)

Fig. 83-9. Battle-axes
(Guui-dong Fort in Seoul, Seoul National University Museum)

Fig. 84-1. Shields
(Corridor mural, eastern side of the burial chamber, Anak Tomb No. 3 in Anak, North Korea)

Fig. 84-2. Helmet
(Fort No. 4 on Mt. Achasan in Seoul, Seoul National University Museum)

Fig. 84-3. Armor suit pieces
(Fort No. 4 on Mt. Achasan in Seoul, Seoul National University Museum)

Fig. 85-1. Armored cavalry
(Corridor mural, eastern side of the burial chamber, Anak Tomb No. 3 in Anak, North Korea)
With long spears in their left hands, cavalry wearing *jongjangpanju* (helmet), *sugap* (gauntlets), and *gyeongap* (spaulders) advance on armored horses.

Fig. 85-2. Armored cavalry
(Mural on the east wall of the antechamber, Deokheung-ri Mural Tomb in Nampo, North Korea)

Fig. 86-1. Battle (replica)
(Mural on the north wall of the first burial chamber, Samsilchong in Ji'an,

China)

The harsh reality of the battle between two camps is well depicted in scenes such as the man-to-man fighting between the two infantry soldiers shown outside of the castle on the left, the mounted combat between the two cavalry shown on the right and the terrified expression of a person gazing out from the fortress. The two soldiers on horseback are iron cavalry whose horses are even armored and helmeted. The pursuer is poised to spear the man in front of him, while the pursued flees in haste half-turned to look at his pursuer. This scene captures the tension of the moment when life and death hangs in the balance.

Fig. 86-2. Beheading

(Mural on the north wall of the burial chamber, northern chamber of Tonggu Tomb No. 12 in Ji'an, China)

Defeat in battle leads only to death. An armored knight (騎士) is about to strike off the head of a defeated soldier which he holds by the helmet. The luster of the sword's blade distinctly contrasts the brightness of the winner and the darkness of the defeated.

Fig. 87. Sanseongha Tombs in Ji'an, China

Fig. 88. Jechong in Ji'an, China

Fig. 89-1. Stele of King Gwanggaeto the Great in Ji'an, China (1920s)

Around 1875, an immense stone monument was discovered in Ji'an, China. In order to reveal the characters inscribed on this 6.39-meter-high stele, an amateur Chinese epigrapher Guan Yueshan applied cow dung to the monument, covered with vines and moss, and lit it on fire. Unfortunately, as some characters chipped during this process, as many as 150 characters out of the total 1,775 could not be identified.

At the stele's head is engraved: "Of old, when our first ancestor King Chumo laid the foundations of our state, he was born in Northern Buyeo as the son of the Heavenly Emperor. His mother, the daughter of Habaek, the god of river... Gukgangsang Gwanggaetogyeong Pyeonganhotaewang (full name of King Gwanggaeto the Great), the seventeenth king, acceded to the throne at the age of 18 and was named Great King Yeongnak. His gracious beneficence reached to Heaven and his majestic military prowess spread to the whole world..." This monument confirmed King Gwanggaeto the Great had expanded Goguryeo's territory, establishing hegemony in northeast Asia.

Carved from hardened lava stone, the stele was erected in 414 and delineates the following in palm-size Chinese characters: the sacred lineage of the Goguryeo royal family, King Gwanggaeto the Great's accomplishments, the monument's maintenance, and other information. It proved very difficult to obtain rubbings of the engraving because of the unevenness of the surface. For that reason, experts filled the empty spots with lime mortar to smooth out the surface before making a rubbing, and were thus able to identify the inscription.

Fig. 89-2. Stele of King Gwanggaeto the Great in Ji'an, China (2000s)

Fig. 90. Reconstruction of Fort No. 4 on Mt. Achasan in Seoul (Choi, Jong-taek)

Fig. 91-1. Gogeomji Mountain Fortress in Liaoning, China

Fig. 91-2. Deungnisa Mountain Fortress in Liaoning, China

Chronological Timeline

The Chronological Timeline of East Asia during Goguryeo

	Goguryeo	Gojoseon, Silla, Baekje, Gaya	East Asia
BC	82 BC Goguryeo people defeat Zhenfan and Lintun commanderies. 37 BC Jumong founds Goguryeo in Jolbon. 36 BC Jumong annexes the state of Biryu and renames it Damuldo (多勿都).	ca. 194 BC Widynasty is founded in Gojoseon. ca. 190 BC Gojoseon incorporates Zhenfan and Lintun commanderies. 108 BC When Gojoseon is conquered by Han Dynasty, some Gojoseon refugees migrate to the southern part of Korean peninsula. 57 BC Six clans of Saro install Bak Hyeokgeose as the first king of Silla. 18 BC Onjo founds Baekje in Wiryeseong.	206 BC Han Dynasty is founded. 108 BC Han conquers Gojoseon and establishes commanderies. 97 BC Sima Qian (司馬遷) of the Han Dynasty completes his *Shiji* (史記, Records of the Grand Historian). 75 BC Han constructs the Xuantu Commandery in Liaodong. 2 BC Buddhism is introduced into Han from the kingdom of Darouzhi (Great Yuezhi).

	Goguryeo	Gojoseon, Silla, Baekje, Gaya	East Asia
1st Century	3 King Yuri moves the capital from Jolbon to Gungnaeseong. 22 King Daemusin attacks Buyeo and kills King Daeso. 56 King Taejo conquers Eastern Okjeo.	8 King Onjo of Baekje attacks Mahan and incorporates part of Mahan into Baekje. 42 Kim Suro founds Garak (Geumgwan). 56 Kim Alji is born in Gyerim, Silla. 85 King Giru of Baekje attacks Silla.	8 Xin (新) Dynasty is established in China. 23 Xin ceases to exist. 25 Later Han is established and Emperor Guangwu ascends the throne. 57 The state of Nakoku (near present-day Fukuoka, Japan 倭奴國) brings tribute to Later Han.
2nd Century	105 King Taejo attacks six prefectures in Liaodong of Later Han. 118 King Taejo invades the Xuantu Commandery of Later Han. 121 King Taejo attacks the Liaodong region in Later Han. 146 King Chadae attacks Xianping in Later Han. 165 Prime Minister Myeongnim Dapbu kills King Chadae and King Sindae ascends the throne. 172 Myeongnim Dapbu defeats Later Han forces in Jwawon.	132 Baekje constructs Bukhan Mountain Fortress. 158 Silla opens the road through Jungnyeong pass.	105 Cai Lun of Later Han develops paper for practical use. 107 King Suisyou (帥升) of Wa brings tribute to Later Han. 172 Geng Lin, the governor of Xuantu of Later Han, attacks Goguryeo. 184 Yellow Turban Rebellion arises in Later Han. 196-ca. 215 The Wudoumi (五斗米教) Taoism, the first Taoist religious sect in China, spreads across Later Han.

	Goguryeo	Gojoseon, Silla, Baekje, Gaya	East Asia
2nd Century	191 King Gogukcheon appoints Eulpaso as prime minister. 194 King Gogukcheon enacts the Jindaebeop (Relief Loan Law). 197 King Sansang ascends the throne. 198 Goguryeo constructs the Hwando Mountain Fortress.		
3rd Century	244 King Dongcheon is defeated by Guanqiu Jian, imperial inspector of Youzhou of Wei (魏) and Hwando Mountain Fortress falls. 259 Goguryeo defeats the Wei army at Yangmaekgok. 300 Prime Minister Changjori dethrones King Bongsang and enthrones Eulbul (King Micheon).	260 King Goi of Baekje establishes the system of six *jwapyeong* (ministers) and 16 ranks of officials. 262 Michu Isageum ascends the throne in Silla. 285 Wang In of Baekje delivers the Thousand Character Classic to Japan. 298 Goguryeo and Nangnang armies kill King Chaekgye of Baekje.	208 Liu Bei and Zhao Zhao meet in the battle of Red Cliffs, also known as the battle of Chibi (赤壁). 205 Gongsun Kang separates the southern half of the Nangnang Commandery to establish the Daifang Commandery. 220 Later Han falls. Wei (魏) is founded. 238 Wei destroys the Gongsun family. 239 Queen Himiko of Japan sends envoys to Wei. 244 Guanqiu Jian, imperial inspector of Youzhou of Wei invades Goguryeo and attacks

	Goguryeo	Gojoseon, Silla, Baekje, Gaya	East Asia
3rd Century			the Hwando Mountain Fortress. 245 Guanqiu Jian invades Goguryeo again. 266 Iyo (壹與) of Japan brings tribute to Jin (晉). 280 Jin defeats Wu (吳) and unifies China.
4th Century	302 King Micheon attacks the Xuantu Commandery. 313 King Micheon conquers the Lelang Commandery. 314 King Micheon conquers the Daifang Commandery. 315 King Micheon attacks the Xuantu Fortress. 335 The Sinseong fortress is built in the former Xuantu Commandery. 342 The Hwando Mountain Fortress falls to an invasion by Former Yan (前燕) and 50,000 prisoners are taken to Former Yan. 355 Goguryeo brings tribute to Former Yan. 357 Anak Tomb No. 3 is constructed. 369 King Gogugwon attacks	304 An assassin sent by Lelang kills King Bunseo of Baekje. 346 King Geunchogo ascends the throne in Baekje. Former Yan attacks Buyeo, taking 50,000 prisoners. 356 Naemul Maripgan ascends the throne in Silla. 371 Baekje moves the capital to Hansan. King Geunchogo and Prince Geungusu attack Goguryeo. Baekje sends *chiljido* (seven-branched sword) to Japan. 375 Ko Heung, a scholar in Baekje, compiles the Baekje history titled *Seogi*. 382 Naemul Maripgan of Silla sends a messenger to Former Qin (前秦).	316 Western Jin (西晉) disintegrates, beginning the Sixteen Kingdoms era which lasts in northern China until 439. 317 Eastern Jin (東晉) is established in Jiangnan (江南). 336 Murong Huang of the Xianbei tribe defeats his younger brother Murong Ren. Tong Shou and Song Huang seek refuge in Goguryeo. 337 Murong Huang assumes the title of "Prince of Yan," establishing Former Yan. 339-342 Former Yan attacks Goguryeo and destroys the Hwando Mountain Fortress. 351 Former Qin (前秦) is

	Goguryeo	Gojoseon, Silla, Baekje, Gaya	East Asia
4th century	Baekje and is defeated in the battle of Chiyang.	384 The foreign monk Marananta (胡僧) arrives from Eastern Jin to propagate Buddhism.	established.
	371 King Gogugwon dies in the battle of Pyeongyangseong and King Sosurim ascends the throne.	392 Silla sends hostages to Goguryeo.	353 The construction of the Thousand Buddha Cave begins in Dunhuang.
	372 A messenger from Fu Jian, the emperor of Former Qin, and the monk Shundao arrive in Goguryeo.	397 Baekje concludes a friendship treaty with Japan and sends Prince Jeonji to Japan as a hostage.	370 Former Yan ends. 372 Fu Jian (苻堅), the emperor of Former Qin, introduces Buddhism into Goguryeo.
	373 King Sosurim promulgates a code of administrative law.	400 The allied army of Gaya and Japan unsuccessfully besieges the Silla fortress, Geumseong. Garagukseong fortress falls to the Goguryeo army.	376 Former Qin unifies northern China.
	391 King Gwanggaeto the Great ascends the throne. Nine Buddhist temples are constructed in Pyeongyang.		383 Eastern Jin defeats Former Qin in the battle of Feishui. Northern China once again is fragmented.
	392 King Gwanggaeto captures over ten Baekje fortresses.		400 Murong Sheng, the king of Later Yan, invades Goguryeo and attacks two fortresses, Sinseong and Namsoseong.
	395 King Gwanggaeto subjugates Biryeo.		
	396 King Gwanggaeto attacks Baekje and King Asin of Baekje surrenders to Goguryeo.		
	400 King Gwanggaeto comes to Silla's aid with an		

	Goguryeo	Gojoseon, Silla, Baekje, Gaya	East Asia
4th Century	army of 50,000 soldiers, keeping an army stationed in Geumseong, Silla.		
5th Century	404 King Gwanggaeto attacks Later Yan. He annihilates the allied army of Baekje and Japan. 408 The Deokheung-ri Mural Tomb is constructed. 410 King Gwanggaeto conquers Eastern Buyeo. 413 King Gwanggaeto dies and King Jangsu ascends the throne. 414 The tombstone of King Gwanggaeto is erected. 427 King Jangsu moves the Goguryeo capital to Pyeongyang. 436 The Goguryeo army is dispatched to Longcheng (龍城) of Northern Yan and returns with a refugee caravan. 438 King Jangsu refuses the request by Liu Song of the Southern Dynasties to send	402 Silla concludes a friendship treaty with Japan and sends Misaheun as a hostage. 417 In Silla, Silseong Maripgan is killed and Nulji Maripgan ascends the throne. 418 Bak Je-sang of Silla helps Silla people held hostage in Goguryeo and Japan to escape. 433 Baekje and Silla form an alliance. 450 The lord of Haseula of Silla kills Byeonjang of Goguryeo. 458 Baekje requests Liu Song to confirm appointment 11 generals. 470 Silla constructs a mountain wall over the course of three years.	413 The king of Wa visits Eastern Jin. 420 Eastern Jin ceases to exist. Liu Song Dynasty (劉宋) is established. 421, 425 San (讚), the king of Wa, visits the Court of Liu Song. 430 The king of Wa visits the Court of Liu Song. 436 Northern Yan falls, Feng Hong (馮弘), the emperor of Northern Yan, and his party seek refuge in Goguryeo. 438 Chin (珍), the king of Wa, visits the Court of Liu Song. 439 Northern Wei (魏) destroys Later Yan and unifies northern China, signaling the start of the era of the Southern and Northern

	Goguryeo	Gojoseon, Silla, Baekje, Gaya	East Asia
5th Century	back Feng Hong, the king of Northern Yan, and kill him. 450 As punishment for the murder of Byeonjang (邊將), King Jangsu dispatches an army to Silla's western border. 468 King Jangsu attacks the Silla fortress Siljikseong with an army of 10,000 Mohe soldiers. 475 King Jangsu subjugates the Baekjae fortress Hanseong and kills King Gaero of Baekje. ca. 480 King Jangsu erects Jungwon Goguryeo monument. 484 The allied forces of Silla-Baekje at Mosanseong fortress defeat Goguryeo army. 494 King Munja provides refuge for the royal family of Buyeo after the Wuji (勿吉) attack. 495 Goguryeo army besieges the Baekje fortress	472 Baekje requests Wei (魏) to attack Goguryeo. 475 In Baekje, King Munju ascends the throne after the fall of Hanseong fortress and moves the capital to Ungjin. 477 In Baekje, the general Hae Gu kills King Munju and enthrones King Samgeun. 479 King Haji of the Garak sends envoys to Southern Qi (南齊). 487 In Silla, Soji Maripgan constructs a new palace in Naeul. 498 King Dongseong of Baekje incorporates the kingdom of Tamna (Jeju Island today).	Dynasties. 443, 451 Sai (讚), the king of Wa, visits Liu Song. 463-476 Bu (武), the king of Wa, visits Liu Song. 468 Wei (魏) attacks Liu Song of the Southern Dynasties. 478 King Bu of Wa sends a memorial to Liu Song to announce his intention to conquer Goguryeo. 479 The Southern Qi Dynasty becomes the second of the Southern Dynasties. King Bu of Wa visits the Court of Qi.

	Goguryeo	Gojoseon, Silla, Baekje, Gaya	East Asia
5th Century	Chiyangseong but is forced to withdraw due to Silla's military intervention. 496 Goguryeo army attacks the Silla fortress Usanseong but is defeated by the Silla army.		
6th Century	537 Goguryeo repels the invasion of the Turks. 548 Goguryeo attacks Baekje but Silla comes to Baekje's aid. 551 Goguryeo loses the Hangang river basin to Silla and Baekje. 554 King Yangwon attacks the Baekje fortress Ungcheonseong. 586 King Pyeongwon moves the palace to the Janganseong fortress. 590 General Ondal dies in the battle of the Acha Mountain Fortress. 598 Goguryeo army attacks the Liaoxi region of Sui (隋) together with the Mohe army.	501 King Dongseong of Baekje is assassinated and King Muryeong ascends the throne. 502 Silla's ruler Jijeung Maripgan prohibits the burial of living persons with the dead. 503 Jijeung Maripgan of Silla formally renames the state Silla and adopts the title of *wang*(king) instead of the title *maripgan*. King Muryeong of Baekje sends envoys to Japan. 512 Isabu of Silla conquers the kingdom of Usan. 514 In Silla, King Jijeung dies and King Beopheung ascends the throne. 520 King Beopheung of Silla promulgates a code of	534 Northern Wei is replaced by Eastern Wei (東魏). 535 Western Wei (西魏) is established. 538 King Seong of Baekje introduces Buddhism to Japan. 550 Eastern Wei is defeated and Northern Qi established. 557 Liang (梁) ceases to exist and Chen (陳) is established. 587 In Japan, Soga no Umako (蘇我馬子) attacks the Mononobe clan (物部氏). 589 Sui (隋) unifies China. 592 In Japan, Soga no Umako has Emperor Sushun assassinated and Empress Suiko ascends the throne.

	Goguryeo	Gojoseon, Silla, Baekje, Gaya	East Asia
6th Century		administrative law.	
		521 King Muryeong sends envoys to Liang informing that Baekje has become a strong country again.	
		523 In Baekje, King Muryeong dies and King Seong ascends the throne.	
		525 In Baekje, the royal tomb of King Muryeong is constructed.	
		527 King Beopheung of Silla officially recognizes Buddhism.	
		532 Geumgwan Gaya surrenders to Silla.	
		536 King Beopheung of Silla establishes an era name and refers to the year as the first year of Geonwon.	
		538 King Seong of Baekje moves the capital to Sabi and renames the kingdom as Nambuyeo (Southern Buyeo).	
		540 In Silla, King Jinheung ascends the throne.	
		541 Baekje sends envoys to Liang (梁) requesting	

	Goguryeo	Gojoseon, Silla, Baekje, Gaya	East Asia
6th Century		Buddhist scriptures, artisans, and painters. 554 King Seong dies in a battle near the Silla fortress of Gwansanseong. 562 Silla conquers Daegaya, ending the Gaya Federation. 591 Silla rebuilds the Namsan wall. 599 King Beop of Baekje prohibits the killing of living thing.	
7th Century	610 The Buddhist monk Damjing brings painting, paper and ink manufacturing techniques to Japan and draws the wall paintings of Horyuji temple. 612 Ulji Mundeok defeats the Sui army at Salsu. 631 Construction on the Cheolli Jangseong Wall begins (completed in 646). 638 Goguryeo destroys the Silla fortress Chiljungseong. 642 Yeon Gaesomun kills King Yeongnyu and	607 Baekje requests Sui China to attack Goguryeo. 608 Silla requests Sui China to attack Goguryeo. 616 Baekje attacks the Silla fortress Mosanseong. 621 Silla enters into formal diplomatic relations with Japan. 629 Kim Yu-sin, a Silla general, destroys the Nangbiseong fortress in Goguryeo. 632 In Silla, Queen Seondeok ascends the throne. Baekje attacks Silla.	604 In Sui (隋), Emperor Yang ascends the throne. Prince Shotoku of Japan creates Japan's first constitution with 17 articles. 607 Japan dispatches officials to visit Sui. 613 Emperor Yang of Sui prepares to invade Goguryeo again but fails. 614 Sui launches a third and unsuccessful invasion of Goguryeo. 618 Sui disintegrates and the Tang (唐) Dynasty is established.

	Goguryeo	Gojoseon, Silla, Baekje, Gaya	East Asia
7th Century	enthrones Bojang, the king's nephew. 647 Goguryeo repels the second Tang invasion. 648 Goguryeo repels the third Tang invasion. 655 Together with Mohe, and Baekje, Goguryeo attacks Silla. 662 Yeon Gaesomun defeats the Tang army and wreaks great losses at Salsu. 666 Yeon Gaesomum dies and Yeon Namsaeng becomes *daemangniji* (prime minister). 668 Pyeongyangseong fortress falls to the allied Silla-Tang army. Goguryeo is no more. King Bojang, his ministers and people are taken as prisoners to Tang. 668- Armed attempts to restore Goguryeo power are launched in many places. 698 Dae Jo-yeong, the founder of Balhae, defeats the Tang army in the battle	642 King Uija of Baekje destroys the Silla fortress Daeyaseong and captures over 40 other fortresses. Kim Chun-chu's request to Goguryeo for military aid is refused. 647 In Silla, the rebellion of Bidam and Yeomjong arises. 648 Silla requests a relief force from Tang. 650 Silla adopts Tang's era name. 654 In Silla, Kim Chun-chu ascends the throne as King Taejong Muyeol. 655 Kim Yu-sin of Silla attacks the Baekjae fortress Dobicheonseong and requests assistance from Tang. 660 The allied Silla-Tang forces conquer Baekje. King Uija and people are taken as prisoners to Tang. 661 In Silla, King Munmu ascends the throne. 663 Attempts to restore	628 Tang Dynasty unifies China. 637 Tang establishes the Zhengguan (貞觀) Code. 645 Tang launches an unsuccessful attack against the Ansiseong fortress in Goguryeo. Xuanzang (玄奘) writes the *Datang Xiyuji* (大唐西域記, Journey to the Western Regions of the Great Tang Dynasty). In Japan, Taika era reforms take place after a coup d'état. 647 Tang makes a dual-pronged attack against Goguryeo via land and sea. 651 Tang establishes the Yonghui (永徽) Code. 660 Tang conquers Baekje and establishes the Ungjin Dodokbu. 661 Su Dingfang (蘇定方) of Tang besieges the Pyeongyangseong fortress of Goguryeo. 663 Japan's relief force for Baekje is defeated in the

	Goguryeo	Gojoseon, Silla, Baekje, Gaya	East Asia
7th Century	of Cheonmullyeong and pronounces the foundation of the Jin state.	Baekje fail due to internal strife. Some Baekje resistance forces flee to Japan. 670 The war between Silla and Tang begins. 675 Silla expands its boundary to the southern end of Goguryeo and establishes military outposts in what had been Baekje territory. 676 Silla repels the Tang army from the southern part of the Daedonggang river and completes its war to unify the peninsula. 679 Silla attacks Tamna (Jeju Island today).	battle at Baekcheon river. 668 Tang conquers Goguryeo and establishes the Andong Dohobu in Pyeongyang. 672 The Jinsin (壬申) war of succession takes place in Japan. 682 The Turks restore their empire. 690 Empress Dowager Wu ascends the Tang throne and renames the dynasty Zhou. 700 The Taiho (大宝) Code is promulgated in Japan.

References

Jeon, Ho-Tae. 1993. "Jangcheon 1 hobun byeokhwa-ui seoyeokgye inmul" (People from Western Regions in the Mural of Jangcheon Tomb No. 1). *Ulsan sahak 6*.

_____. 1999. *Gobun byeokhwa-ro bon goguryeo iyagi* (Goguryeo History as Seen through Tomb Murals). Pulbit.

_____. 2000. *Goguryeo gobun byeokhwa yeongu* (Goguryeo Tomb Murals). Sakyejul.

_____. 2004a. *Byeokhwayeo goguryeo-reul malhara* (Mural Paintings, Talking about Goguryeo). Sakyejul.

_____. 2004b. "5 segi pyeongyanggwon gobun byeokhwa-ro bon goguryeo munhwa-ui jeongcheseong" (Goguryeo Cultural Identity through Tomb Murals in the 5th Century Pyeongyang). *Goguryeo yeongu* (Goguryeo Research) 18.

_____. 2004c. *Goguryeo gobun byeokhwa-ui segye* (The World of Goguryeo Mural Paintings). Seoul National University Press.

_____. 2007. *The Dreams of the Living and Hopes of the Dead*. Seoul National University Press.

Kang, Sun. 2001. "Goguryeo-wa jeonyeon-ui gwangye-e daehan gochal" (Review on Relations between Goguryeo and Former Yan). *Goguryeo yeongu* (Goguryeo Research) 11.

Kong, Seok-koo. 1998. *Goguryeo yeongyeok hwakjangsa yeongu* (History of Goguryeo Expansion). Seogyeong Munhwasa.

Lee, Jong-wook. 1987. "Goguryeo chogi-ui jeongchijeok seongjang-gwa daejungguk gwangye" (Early Goguryeo's Political Development and its Relations with China). In *Dongasa-ui bigyo yeongu* (Comparative Study on East Asian History). Ilchokak.

Lee, Seong-je. 2000. "Yeongyangwang 9 nyeon goguryeo-ui yoseo gonggyeok" (Goguryeo's Attack against Liaoxi in the 9th Year of King Yeongyang's Reign). *Jindan hakbo* (Journal of the Jindan Historical Society) 90.

_____. 2001. "Goguryeo-wa bukje-ui gwangye" (Relations between Goguryeo and Northern Qi). *Hanguk godaesa yeongu* (Korean Old History Study) 23.

_____. 2004. "Goguryeo jangsuwang-ui daebugwi gyoseop-gwa geu jeongchijeok uimi" (King Jangsu's Policy on Northern Wei and its Political Significance). *Yeoksa hakbo* (Journal of History) 181.

Lim, Ki-hwan. 2004. *Goguryeo jeongchisa yeongu* (A Study of the Political History of Goguryeo). Saenarae.

Noh, Tae-don. 1981. "Goguryeo yuminsa yeongu" (A Study of Migration History of Goguryeo). In *Han Woo-geun baksa jeongnyeon ginyeom sahak nonchong* (Collection of Treaties to Commemorate the Retirement of Dr. Han Woo-geun). Jisik Sanup Publishing.

_____. 1981. "Yeon Gaesomun and Kim Chun-chu." *Hanguksa simin gangjwa* (The Citizens' Forum on Korean History) 5.

_____. 1999. *Goguryeosa yeongu* (A Study of Goguryeo History). Sakyejul.

Park, Han-je. 1998. *Jungguk jungse hohan cheje yeongu* (On the Sino-Barbarian Synthesis in Medieval China). Ilchokak.

Suh, Yeong-dae. 2003. "Goguryeo-ui gukga jesa" (State Rites of Goguryeo). *Hanguksa yeongu* (Korean History Research) 120.

Yang, Byeong-ryong. 1997. "Nadang jeonjaeng jinhaeng gwajeong-e boineun goguryeo yumin-ui daedang tujaeng" (Goguryeo Refugees' Resistance against Tang during the Silla-Tang War). *Sachong* (Journal of the Historical Society of Korea) 46.

Yeo, Ho-kyu. 1995. "3 segi goguryeo-ui sahoe byeondong-gwa tongchi cheje-ui byeonhwa" (Changes in Society and Ruling System in Third Century Goguryeo). *Yeoksa-wa hyeonsil* (History and Reality) 15.

_____. 1996. "Amnokgang jungnyu yuyeok-eseo goguryeo-ui gukga hyeongseong" (The Formation of Goguryeo in the Middle Amnokgang River Basin). *Yeoksa-wa hyeonsil* (History and Reality) 21.

_____. 1999. "Goguryeo hugi-ui gunsa bangeo chegyewa gunsa jeollyak" (Defense System and Military Strategy of Late Goguryeo). *Hanguk gunsasa yeongu* (Korean Military History Study) 3.

井上直樹. 2000.「高句麗の對北魏外交と朝鮮半島情勢」.『朝鮮史研究會論文集』38.

Index